BORN TO WIN

BORN TO WIN

YOU CAN TURN YOUR DREAMS INTO REALITY.

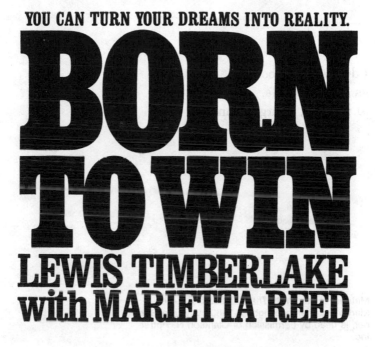

BORN TO WIN

LEWIS TIMBERLAKE
with MARIETTA REED

**Tyndale House
Publishers, Inc.
Wheaton, Illinois**

I dedicate this book,
as I have my life,
to my wife, Georgia Ann.

Second printing, January 1987

Library of Congress Catalog Card Number 85-52331
ISBN 0-8423-0338-3
Copyright © 1986 by Lewis Timberlake and Marietta Reed
All rights reserved
Printed in the United States of America

CONTENTS

PREFACE

I don't understand. . . .

. . . how a black cow can eat green grass which turns into white milk and yellow butter.

. . . how a caterpillar encases itself in its homemade casket and changes into a beautiful butterfly; how its hair changes into scales (one million to a square inch); how its many legs become the six legs of the butterfly; and how its yellow color turns into a brilliant red.

. . . how a handful of sand deposited in the heart of the earth is miraculously changed into a fiery opal when heat is applied from beneath and ponderous weight from above.

. . . how a handful of black carbon planted deep in the bowels of the earth is transformed into a glorious diamond fit for a king's crown when that same heat and weight are applied.

7

. . . how oxygen and hydrogen (both of them odorless, tasteless, and colorless) can combine with black, insoluble, tasteless carbon to become sweet, white sugar.

. . . how the human heart, only six inches in length and four inches in diameter, can beat 70 times per minute, 4,200 times per hour, 100,800 times per day, 36,792,000 times per year, and 2,575,440,000 times in an average lifetime.

. . . how that same tiny heart could be so successful that, every time it beats, it pumps blood at a rate of 2.5 ounces per beat, 175 ounces per minute, 656 pounds per hour, and 7.75 tons per day!

. . . why some people are born with so little and yet achieve so much.

. . . why some who have so much seem to accomplish so very little.

All of my life I've been intrigued by life's questions and driven to find the answers. It has been a joy and a privilege to be involved in this quest. I'm grateful to those who over the years have helped, encouraged, and inspired me. I'm refreshed by those who have given their lives to similar pursuits; especially those who have been so willing to share their ideas, information, and discoveries with me.

I appreciate those with whom I've worked so closely through the years. To them I express my thanks and openly admit that this book is a product of their labors. Their commitment to heal human suffering and encourage greater personal growth among human beings has made this book possible.

I am moved by the talent of Marietta Reed, whose love for people is exceeded only by her ability to transform the spoken word into written guidelines for life.

Above all, I must express my thanks to my wife, Georgia Ann, who has been my companion, my joy, my inspiration, my strength, my comfort, and my friend.

Lewis R. Timberlake

INTRODUCTION

A strange new society is moving in upon us. The "future shock" described by Alvin Toffler in his book by the same name is here today. We're living in an incredible time of change—a time when human history has made a sharp break with all past human experience. This change is bringing emotion-filled options to millions of men and women—options so new and strange that past experience will no longer offer clues to dealing with the new problems which this change will present.

The information explosion which has occurred within the past one hundred years is phenomenal. If you stacked a dime upon a dime upon a dime until you had a stack of dimes as tall as the Washington Monument, the first dime would represent knowledge as we know it today. The rest of the stack would represent knowledge which will be acquired in our lifetime. Major library holdings must double every sixteen years just to keep up with new knowledge. Experts tell us that by the year 2040, Yale University will need over eight acres of land just to accommodate its library.

Obsolescence among today's scientists, physicians, and engineers is a very real problem. In 1950 the chemical world published 558 articles every two weeks covering the latest advances in chemistry. Today chemists publish 6,700 articles every two weeks. Cable Health Network reported in the spring of 1984 that 90 percent of all scientists who ever lived are alive and working today. These people control our future and have the awesome responsibility of remaining up to date in the ever-changing world of science and technology.

We live in a time when today's traveler can go from New York to Moscow in less time than it took George Washington to travel from New York to Philadelphia. We live in a time in which one generation has witnessed travel evolve from horse-drawn buggies to motor cars to airplanes, and finally to space exploration and the placement of men on the moon.

This same generation has seen simple arithmetic evolve into a strange "new math." It has seen simple electricity evolve into advanced electronics, giving us computer technology and the massive Univac computer large enough to fill an entire room. From this has come microelectronics, enabling us to put a computer on our wrists and providing video games and small desk-top computers for our homes. This continuing evolution of technology will, no doubt, someday make the placement of astronauts on the moon look primitive in comparison.

If we're to survive the stress and change of this knowledge explosion, we must become infinitely more adaptable and capable of solving problems, making decisions, setting and working toward goals, communicating with other people in addition to our families, and understanding who we are and what we want out of life.

We look where we've been and question whether it's been worthwhile. We look at where we are now, wondering what our purpose in life is and where we're going with it. The future is unknown and frightening. We think of tomorrow, of the tomorrows after tomorrow, yearning for a sense of fulfillment, for a meaningful direction to our lives, and for a renewed sense of awareness and self-realization.

We look at successful people and ask, "How did they do that?" How do some people succeed and become prosperous while others with the same capabilities and talents don't? Why do some people try so hard and never seem to reach the dreams that they earnestly desire and deserve? Why do so few people seem to find the readily available path to success?

In the following pages, I hope to show each of you a way to know who you are, what you want out of life, and a way to go about getting those things you want and dream about. If you can discover who you are and what your life's goals are, you'll have the basis for self-improvement, coping, and growth. Some people learn through experience, others through the help of a counselor, pastor, friend, or relative. Insight usually comes in bits and pieces over the years.

A person must be willing to adapt to the changes going on around him. A person must be willing to recognize that stability requires change and adaptation in a changing environment. A person must be willing to pay the price to do the things that unsuccessful people won't do—things that won't compromise beliefs, convictions, and values. There is a cost involved when one is actively pursuing and eventually achieving his or her life's goals. But so few people are willing to pay the price that success demands. Why?

Dr. Maxwell Maltz, noted author and physician, has said that every single person is born with the right to be successful, but that we gradually lower our standards for success until we finally settle for mediocrity.

> Some people short-change themselves and never reach their full share of possible accomplishments, or their full potential as human beings. If you emphasize your negative qualities and fail to appreciate your assets, [you can] do something about it. If you are willing to exert effort in the best cause you'll ever have, you'll learn to be fair to yourself.[1]

For example, it's not what happens to you, but how you *react* to what happens that separates the winners from the losers, and successful from the unsuccessful. Winston Churchill once said, "Things don't happen to me. I happen to things!" Successful people are simply willing to pay the price and do the things that are necessary in order to achieve their dreams and their goals. These necessary steps to success can be taken without hurting other people in the process and without compromising one's beliefs and convictions.

As human beings, we're motivated by our needs and deterred by our fears. We're told to work hard, dream big dreams, and success will follow. But success demands more than working hard and dreaming big. It requires a *belief* in yourself as a human being. This includes a belief in your God-given talents, capabilities, desires, goals, and dreams. Psychological research has shown that if you *believe* in yourself and in your goals, your mind will be the motivator, the key to almost anything you desire.

The brain and the nervous system constitute a marvelous and complex goal-striving mechanism—a sort of built-in automatic guidance system—which can work for you as a success mechanism or against you as a failure mechanism. It all depends on how you, the operator, operate it; on what you tell it about yourself; and on the goals you set for it. If you program it positively and act accordingly, it will respond for you in extraordinary ways.

> God brought us forth on this earth to live, not to stagnate. He meant us to be happy, to enjoy our lives. He meant us to relish every moment, to weave loving care on every day that we live, no matter how young or how old we are. Happiness is a habit, just as brushing your teeth or washing your face. You can acquire this habit. If you have been conditioned to feel sour about yourself and your world, you can change; you can take hold of this habit of happiness.[2]

The way we look upon ourselves is called our self-image. Our self-image is acquired through a lifetime of experiences, successes, and failures. It's formed from earliest childhood and is affected by how we see others viewing us, by what we think others expect of us, by what we think society expects of us, and by our relationships with others, including God. Over the years we gain an opinion of ourselves, whether it's accurate or not, from what we've been told by our parents, teachers, and friends.

Dr. Joyce Brothers says that the self-image sets the boundaries of individual accomplishment. It defines what you can and cannot do. Expand the self-image and you have more possibilities. Maltz writes,

> To live in reality, an individual must like himself—as he really is. If you distrust yourself, if you are ashamed of yourself, if you can't live with yourself, then you will try to be somebody else. . . . A healthy self-image is your key toward achieving life in reality.[3]

You must find yourself acceptable to *you* and still be willing to grow as a person.

Growth is being able to see change in yourself. Growth is knowing you're different today from yesterday, but still partly the same. Growth is adding knowledge, using it, and being able to cope with the change going on around you. Growth is increasing your abilities to communicate and contribute. Growth is setting goals for change and achieving them. Growth is recognizing that stability requires change in a changing world. Growth is moving a bit closer to being yourself—a person with all the opposites contained in the whole. Growth is discovering who you are and liking what you've found.

The ability to know and understand your own behavior is one of the most important aspects of getting the most living out of life, adapting to the world around you, and setting and achieving your life's goals. The objective of this book is to help you discover your God-given talents and abilities— those talents and abilities that an inaccurate self-image may be masking. Along these same lines, this book will help you discover who you are, presenting a program wherein you can understand yourself, cope with the world around you, and set and achieve your life's goals.

By reading this book you will learn the reasons why people fail. You will realize that you have the potential to be more productive, more positive, and more profitable to yourself, your business, and your family. You will discover the power to overcome obstacles, surpass overwhelming odds, come back from disheartening failures, and persevere when others quit. You'll learn how you can become the man or woman you want to be—and have a right to be. And consequently, you'll learn how you can have the dreams and desires of your heart.

God didn't create you, engineer you for success, and then let you dream dreams of achievement in order to taunt you. You have to choose less than God's best for you not to be the man or woman you want to be and were created to be. God gave you talents and abilities to use, not to waste. The program outlined in this book is nothing more than a detailed approach to how you can come to know yourself better. In addition, this approach includes setting and achieving your life's goals, and showing you how you can do what it takes in order to become successful. *Anyone can be a winner!*

PART ONE
WINNING & LOSING

PART ONE
WINNING
& LOSING

1
"HOW'D THEY DO THAT?"

THE WHITE-HAIRED, eighty-eight-year-old gentleman wasn't a very good speaker. He simply stood on the stage and answered questions from the audience for forty-five minutes. When he finished, the audience gave him a standing ovation, cheering him as he slowly walked off the stage, aided only by a shiny silver cane. Just to be on the same program with this man excited me because I'd admired him for years.

As the old man laboriously hobbled down the steps, a shout rang out from the California audience of six thousand realtors, "I've got one more question for you, sir. Could you tell us your secret of success?"

The audience grew silent as it waited for his words of wisdom. The old gentleman slowly turned and said, "Remember that young man who spoke right ahead of me?"

That was me—a young man. I liked that!

"That's the secret," he continued. "Your answer lies in the things he told you."

I could hardly wait to meet him. Fortunately for me, he was booked on my flight home from California to Dallas, where I changed planes for Austin and he continued on his journey. We had a lot of time to talk during that trip. He shared some interesting thoughts with me about his life.

His father had died when he was only five years old. He quit school when he was a young man of sixteen. By age seventeen he'd already lost four jobs. He was married at eighteen, and before he was nineteen he became a father. When he was twenty his wife left him and took their baby daughter with her. Between the ages of eighteen and twenty-two he worked as a railroad conductor and failed, joined the Army and washed out there, farmed some land and couldn't succeed at that, applied for law school and was rejected, and became an insurance salesman and failed again. This man couldn't do anything! The only thing he found that he could do well was cook. So he became a cook and dishwasher in a small cafe—not a glamorous life.

He had a lot of time to think while working long hours in that small hot cafe. He grieved for his wife and baby daughter. He begged his wife to return to him, but she refused. Oh, if he could only get his little daughter back! He loved her and missed her so much.

He spent a lot of time formulating a plan to get his daughter back, meticulously mapping out everything in his mind, calculating every move. For a week, this young grief-stricken father lay in the bushes outside his wife's small house, watching his daughter play and planning his next move. He would kidnap her!

The day came for him to execute his fail-safe plan. He was nervous, excited, and frightened. Driven by love, he once again positioned himself in the bushes, watching for his daughter to come out and play. That was the one day she didn't come outside. He'd even failed at committing a crime! He told me he felt he was the ultimate loser, a nobody, destined to be alone for the rest of his life.

Eventually he was able to convince his wife to return home. Together they worked in the cafe, cooking and washing dishes, until he retired at age sixty-five. On his first day of retirement he went to the post office. There he found a letter from the United States government. He opened it and inside found his first Social Security check for $105.00. It seemed as though the government was saying he couldn't take care of himself anymore; that all he could do was exist for the rest of his days on its support.

It wasn't the first time the old gentleman had felt dejected, defeated, demoralized, and discouraged. His life had been one disappointment after another for sixty-five long years. So he decided that if he couldn't take care of himself, if the government had to take care of him, his life wasn't worth living. He would commit suicide.

Taking a piece of paper and a pencil, he walked out behind his house and sat down under a spreading shade tree, planning to write his last will and testament. Instead, for the very first time in his life, he began to write down what he should be, what he'd planned for in his life, and what he would like to do with his remaining years. He discovered that he wasn't through yet! There *was* something he could do that no one else he knew could do as well. He knew how to cook! He'd spent his entire life behind a hot stove. Then and there he determined that if it killed him, he was going to die trying to be somebody and to do something worthwhile with the rest of his life.

He got up from under the shade tree, went to the bank in his hometown, and borrowed $87 against his next Social Security check. With that $87 he bought some boxes and chicken. Then he went home and fried the chicken in a special recipe which he'd developed over the years in that little cafe. He started selling his chicken door to door in his hometown of Corbin, Kentucky.

That sixty-five-year-old chicken salesman became Colonel Harlan Sanders, beloved king of the Kentucky Fried Chicken empire.

Someone in the audience that day asked, "Colonel Sanders, how much money are you worth?"

"I don't know, son," he quipped. "But if I want it, I can buy it!"

At sixty-five, he was a monumental, lifelong, washed-out

19

failure. At eighty-eight, he was a multimillionaire and had the world by the tail, bowing to standing ovations across the country. How'd he do that?

An attractive, self-assured young lady stood before the Tennessee audience, proud to be honored by her friends and family. A film of her life had just been shown, and she was about to receive one of the highest honors ever bestowed upon someone in her profession.

She was born in 1940 in the rolling hills of St. Bethlehem, Tennessee, four months premature and weighing only 4.5 pounds. Her left leg was shorter than her right, and she spent most of her childhood trying to recover from various ailments.

When she was four years old she contracted both double pneumonia and scarlet fever. Doctors told her mother that daily massage would be necessary to restore the use of her paralyzed leg. So, for the next two years, while she was confined to a wheelchair, her mother and family took turns massaging her leg and driving her ninety miles round-trip to Nashville for heat and water therapy.

During the long nights when her leg ached so much she couldn't sleep, this little child's mother rocked her and crooned songs to her; songs which told of God's love for her and how someday she'd be someone special.

When she reached age eight, she was fitted with a leg brace and could finally walk and attend school like other children. Her classmates nicknamed her "Limpy"; a cruel name which stuck with her all through elementary, junior high, and senior high schools. But Limpy, remembering the days of her early childhood and the songs her mother had sung to her, remained determined to live up to what she and God both knew she could be.

As Limpy was growing up she discovered she loved sports. She could usually be found after school shooting baskets with one of her nineteen brothers and sisters, refusing to allow her disability to hamper her fun. The exercise proved to be as much therapy as pleasure, and at age eleven Limpy was able to discard her leg brace forever.

Two years later, Limpy entered Clarksville High School in

Tennessee and made the basketball team. By age fifteen she was averaging thirty-two points per game, making the all-state team her junior year. Her athletic ability was the primary reason why Clarksville High School established a women's track team. And, of course, she was encouraged to be a part of it.

Limpy excelled in track as she had excelled in basketball. Ed Temple, women's track coach at Tennessee A & I University, saw her run off with the state high school track meet her senior year by winning the 50-, 75-, and 100-yard dashes. He not only liked her ability to run, but was impressed with her determination, self-confidence, and ability to overcome personal obstacles. As a result, he offered her a track scholarship to Tennessee A & I.

At age sixteen, after running high school track for only one year, and as a college freshman, Limpy ran on the 1956 U. S. Olympic team in the 400-meter relay, winning a bronze medal. Four years later, as a college senior, Limpy represented her school in the AAU Championships where she set a world record of 22.9 seconds for the 200 meters.

That same year, her college coach, Ed Temple, was selected to coach the American Olympic women's track team at the summer games in Rome. He immediately chose Limpy as one of the athletes to run on the women's team. One of this country's leading newspapers later ran an article which criticized Coach Temple by saying that he shouldn't even be allowed to coach. It said he was trying to embarrass America by choosing a cripple as one of its representatives, as a symbol of man's inhumanity to man.

But Limpy went to Rome.

The first event in which Limpy participated was the 100 meters. The spectators in the stadium that day saw a race they would never forget. When the race was over the crowd literally went wild. They cheered and stomped their feet, jumping up and down for a crippled black girl from America who had just won the gold medal!

That evening at the medal ceremonies, seventy-three thousand people watched as Limpy stood on the raised platform, lowering her head to accept an amateur athlete's highest honor. As she looked up and saw the American flag rising above the other two and heard the strains of "The Star-Spangled Banner" being played in her honor, a thrill swept over her.

Standing on that platform, basking in the glory of personal achievement, her mind went back to her childhood in the hills of Tennessee, and she thought, "Mamma, you were right! God really does love me! He *really* does! I *am* a winner! I *am* somebody special!"

When it came time to run the 200 meters, Limpy discovered that she had to run against one of Germany's most outstanding women athletes, Jutta Heine. The starter's gun cracked, and the athletes sprinted quickly down the track. With determination in her heart and the sounds of her mother's voice echoing through her mind, Limpy did it again, winning her second gold medal!

This time, as she stood on the platform to accept her gold medal, a different thrill went through her. For the first time since Babe Didrikson competed in the 1932 Olympic Games, an American woman had a chance to win *three* gold medals in track and field!

The news spread through the Olympic village like a grass fire out of control. By the time the 400-meter relay was to begin, Limpy was the talk of the village. The Americans became the odds-on favorites to win over the once-favored German team.

Two hours before race time it was standing room only in the stadium, and the officials had to close the gates to keep out the crowds. The air was full of excitement. People were asking each other if Limpy could do it again. Could the black American girl with the limp win three gold medals in a row?

The crowd grew strangely silent as the runners took their positions in the blocks. Limpy and her three Tennessee A & I teammates had already set a world record of 44.4 seconds in a preliminary heat. The pressure would be on the previously favored German team this time. Both Limpy and her former opponent, Jutta Heine, would run the anchor leg of the relay.

The crack of the start gun broke the silence and they were off. The women sprinted around the first lap, then the second, and then into the third. The tension was quickly building, both on and off the field.

As her teammate approached Limpy to pass off the baton, the crowd went wild, shouting, screaming, and stamping their feet. There was no doubt as to whom they were for. Then silence. The two-yard American lead was quickly lost because of a poor pass of the baton to Limpy by her teammate. . . . Now you and I both know that races are won and lost by mere fractions of a second. The most minute mistake can make all the difference between winning and losing.

After it was over, the reporters in Rome asked Limpy what went through her mind at that moment. She said her very first thought was to crawl into the infield grass and just die. Her second thought was to go home to her Tennessee hills and tell her mother that God didn't love her after all. She wanted to tell her mother that God just lets you get close to glory and then laughs and mocks you as he watches you crumble and fall into the burning flames of failure.

As I sat there that evening and watched the film of this race unfolding before me, I could see Limpy grab at the baton and bobble it. At that instant, it looked as if all emotion drained from her face and life itself simply vanished. In spite of her critical mistake, for some reason the camera stayed right on her face. Suddenly, just as quickly as it had vanished, I could see life coming back into her, flooding her with energy, gripping her and urging her on. Her face took on an expression of purpose and determination. Somehow the baton made its way back into her hand and she began to *run*.

Limpy ran as though her life depended on it, as if she had supernatural energy. She not only caught up with Jutta Heine, but passed her and beat her by three yards to tie the Olympic record of 44.5 seconds. Limpy had won her third gold medal!

She later told reporters that her mother was right, and it was this belief in her own potential that had urged her on. She knew she could do it. She knew that God had created her and loved her, and that he doesn't make mistakes!

In both 1960 and 1961 Limpy was named the Associated Press Female Athlete of the Year. She was also awarded the outstanding amateur athlete's Sullivan Award in 1961. Her coach, Ed Temple, said, "She's done more for her country than the United States could pay her for."

As a baby she was premature, underweight, and crippled. During her childhood she faced years of illness and immobility. As a young woman she was an accomplished athlete, receiving three Olympic gold medals in track and field.

Following her Olympic triumph, Wilma "Limpy" Rudolph received successive awards as the outstanding woman athlete of the year and the amateur athlete's award of 1961. Today she is a respected professional expert in her field and is called upon for commentary and advice. How'd she do that?

An "incorrigible criminal, an unsalvageable human being." These words were once used to describe him. He was born to a black mother who earned her living as a prostitute, and a white father in Longview, Texas, on February 7, 1930. He grew up where crime was a way of life.

"When other kids were shooting marbles, I was following the milkmen and the people who put bread on doorsteps, stealing any food they left behind," he says.

He ran away to New York City at the age of twelve. He ended up shining shoes in Grand Central Station, living among thieves, murderers, and prostitutes.

"What I wanted then," he says, "was somebody to listen to me and someone to understand that I was a person."

Before the Korean War, he enlisted in the military, receiving an honorable discharge in 1951. Within months of his discharge he had run afoul of the law. He was convicted of burglary in 1952 and armed robbery in 1956, and violated his parole both times. He spent a total of seventeen years in the Texas Department of Corrections.

It was while he was in prison that he acquired the nickname "Racehoss"—a name referring to his cotton-chopping skills which he'd developed on the prison farm. After spending a considerable amount of time in solitary confinement, and almost at his row's end, he finally cried out to God for help. And he was answered.

At this turning point in his life, Race resumed his education through the Texas Department of Corrections. He obtained his high school equivalency diploma and moved on to college, where he studied psychological counseling and therapy, heavy equipment engineering, and the humanities. His education also included TDC courses in salesmanship, business management, painting contracting, and map making and architectural blueprints.

Following his release from prison to a halfway house in 1972, Race rose from a reporter to the General Manager of the *Forward Times*—the largest black newspaper in the Southwest, published in Houston. Approximately one year later, Race left the newspaper to join a close friend he'd met in prison and to manage New Directions, a well-known Houston halfway house for ex-offenders.

On December 18, 1973, Race was appointed Director of Project Star (Social Transition and Re-Adjustment), a division of the Governor's Office, Criminal Justice Division. There he coordinated services to those imprisoned for possession of four ounces or less of marijuana. These inmates were being released under the provisions of a new Texas penal code.

Upon termination of this program, Race moved to the Comprehensive Offender Manpower Program, doing much the same work as before, but on a wider scale. COMP gave direct assistance to ex-offenders in all phases of the criminal justice system. Special emphasis was given to expanding the employment opportunities of the ex-offenders.

From there, he went on to become Travis County's first ex-offender adult probation officer and the city of Austin's first ex-offender to serve as a division head for a department. In 1976, Governor Dolph Briscoe gave Race a full pardon.

Race has received awards and recognition for his work in the field of corrections. He was awarded two Services to Mankind Awards in 1975 and Travis County's prestigious Liberty Bell Award in 1977. He was the keynote speaker at the Texas Corrections Association Convention in 1976 and in 1981. After becoming a department head for the city of Austin, he received the Outstanding Crime Prevention Citizen in the State Award for development of ACE (Austin City Employees) Crime Watch Program.

Albert Race Sample has proved that an ex-offender can

make it in the free world. He has come from a fifth-grade education to college studies at the University of Houston, has gone from being a "three-time loser" to a definite winner. He is recognized throughout the criminal justice field for his contributions to the ex-offender. Race Sample's accomplishments are many, but notably he lists one near the top.

"I have learned how to live a normal, productive, respectful life, with dignity and with honesty," he says.

Race Sample has written a book describing his life; a life which seemed to be on a collision course with the penitentiary from the beginning. *Racehoss: Big Emma's Boy,* published in 1984, has met with sensational reviews and was pronounced one of the top fifteen books of 1984 by *The Dallas Morning News*. It is scheduled to be published in paperback by Random House in January 1986.

When he was a child, he lived off the streets. When he was a teenager, he was a criminal and a runaway. He spent seventeen years behind bars, labeled an "incorrigible, unsalvageable human being." Since his release in 1972, he has accomplished more than most people accomplish in a lifetime. How'd he do that?

When most people would have given up and quit, why did Harlan Sanders, Wilma Rudolph, and Race Sample hang on and persevere? How did they overcome personal defeat and surpass overwhelming odds to become the persons they dreamed of becoming? Where does that special drive come from that says, "I have a right to succeed. I *can* be a winner if I only try, if I am willing to pay the price"?

Our Creator didn't place us on this earth to be losers, and he didn't place dreams in our hearts to discourage us. The very fact that we have dreams is proof that we were meant to aspire to greater things, proof that other possibilities exist. Somehow we've been misled along the way. We've been taught that we have no right to be successful, that we're supposed to be satisfied with our "lot in life," and that success must always belong to others. Not so. God intended us to be winners, to use the talents and abilities he's given us to become all that we can be.

A winner isn't necessarily a wealthy person. Success isn't

measured by the number of dollars one has in a bank account, or by a certain number of possessions.

Then what is success? Success is measured by *the price a person is willing to pay* to get "there"; a price that does not ask that a person compromise his or her beliefs and convictions in the process.

And what is a winner? A winner is simply *a man or a woman who has become all that he or she ever dreamed of becoming*, who has accomplished the goals they set out to achieve. *Anyone can be a winner!*

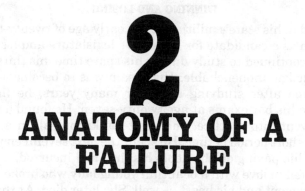

2
ANATOMY OF A FAILURE

NESTLED BACK IN the hills lay a small cabin inhabited by a carpenter and his barely literate wife. They could scarcely eke out a living from carpentry work and wood chopping, their only means of support. So when a son was born to them, it was only natural that the father would eventually train him in carpentry and wood chopping as well.

This tall, lanky boy chopped wood for his father until he was twenty-one. But chopping wood couldn't satisfy his hunger for knowledge, so he borrowed books and read by candlelight during the evening hours. The things he learned in those books planted dreams in his mind of better things, of other occupations, and of other worlds beyond his little country town.

By the time he was twenty-seven, this young man had worked on a Mississippi ferry boat, in a mill, general store, and post office, as a farm hand and a surveyor, and had served in his state's militia. At the early age of twenty-three he ran as a candidate for his state's legislature and lost. He continued to study during his spare time, his thirst for knowledge unquenchable. His dream was to become a lawyer, and after studying alone for many years, he finally passed his bar exams at age twenty-seven. He found a partner, went into practice, and went bankrupt—all in a relatively short period of time. He spent the next seventeen years of his life paying off the debts his firm had incurred.

He fell in love with a beautiful young lady who broke their engagement and his heart as well. She later died. At the age of thirty-three, he finally married a young woman with a strong will and a temper to match. Their marriage proved to be as stormy and volatile as her temper. Of the four sons born to them, three died before reaching adulthood.

At age thirty-five he reopened his law practice. His desire to serve in public office proved as insatiable as his quest for knowledge. Even though he'd lost one election twelve years before, he optimistically sought office again—and lost, again. At age forty-seven, his party selected him as their vice-presidential candidate. Again, he lost. At age forty-nine, he was nominated for the United States Senate, and again he lost.

Here was a man whose formal schooling at age twenty-two totaled less than one year. He lost the love of his life, his law practice, and three sons. He had a rocky and stormy marriage. He sought public office numerous times, only to be defeated time and time again. By anyone's definition of a failure, this man most certainly must have been one.

However, in spite of all those failures, he *did* experience a few successes. At age twenty-five, after having lost a bid for the state legislature, he came back and won, serving four terms. At age thirty-eight, after losing a bid for a Congressional seat three years earlier, he was elected to Congress for one term. And after losing the vice-presidential nomination and a United States Senate seat, he was nominated as the Republican Party's presidential candidate at age fifty-one and won. When he turned fifty-five, he was renominated and reelected to a second presidential term.

History has testified that Abraham Lincoln not only emancipated the slaves; he also became a strong party leader who maintained a faith in democracy that rubbed off on his countrymen. He became a national symbol of man's quest for freedom. And after many failures, he remained undaunted, coming back and changing the course of this nation.

How did he do that? And why do so many fail while so few succeed? I believe there are four major reasons why potential winners end up as hopeless failures in life.

ANTICIPATION OF FAILURE

The number one reason why marriages break up, businesses go under, students fail in school, etc., is *anticipation* of failure. People expect to fail. We're conditioned by the failure around us until we believe we can't possibly be successful. After all, why should we be any different?

According to the U. S. Chamber of Commerce, in 1971, 48.3 percent of the people who borrowed money, took investors, withdrew their life's savings, and/or opened businesses went under within one year. The government gave Dr. Dorothy Stanton a grant to study those businesses and determine the cause of so much failure. After months of study, Stanton reported that 85 percent of all businesses failed because of "anticipation of failure."

In the 1952 summer Olympic games in Helsinki, Finland, the United States had two of the few pole vaulters in the world who had a chance to clear fifteen feet. One of those men had been the world's most consistent performer and was the favorite to win the pole vault that year. Known as the Vaulting Vicar and Reverend Robert, Bob Richards came prepared to set a new Olympic record.

The Olympic record for the pole vault had been set in Berlin in 1936 at 14 feet 3.75 inches. Richards and his teammate both cleared 14 feet 5 inches with ease—but so did athletes from Sweden and Russia. So the bar was boosted up to 14 feet 9.125 inches. Both Americans easily sailed over that height as well.

The bar was raised to 14 feet 11.14 inches. Only Reverend Bob was able to clear that amazing height. The twenty-six-year-old minister and teacher from the University of Illinois had won the Olympic championship without even touching the crossbar. But Bob Richards wanted that magic fifteen-foot mark on his record.

The bar was raised to fifteen feet—a mere fraction of an inch above the height he had just cleared with ease. However, that magic mark was not to be recorded as an accomplishment that year. The Vaulting Vicar failed to achieve his goal for the first time in his life.

During the next four years Bob Richards accumulated more fifteen-foot vaults than any man who ever lived. So when he returned to the Olympics for the second time in Melbourne, Australia, it was presumed by everyone there that he would be the 1956 pole vault champion.

It was to everyone's surprise that this Olympic champion, whose picture had appeared all across America on the front of Wheaties cereal boxes, failed to clear 13 feet 1.5 inches in his first try.

Unshaken, he took his position again and tried his second vault. He seemingly sailed over with ease, but when he landed in the sawdust pit below, he looked up in time to see the bar come crashing down after him. This Olympic champion was one jump away from elimination. Now he was shaken.

He examined his pole, tested the ground, talked to the officials, exercised to loosen up, and changed his clothes. This was ridiculous. He could almost clear thirteen feet without a pole! The bar was raised to 13 feet 7.5 inches. This time he sailed over it with ease.

Now he was over the hurdles. The finals proved to be a relief as he cleared the qualifying heights with no problems. When the pole vaulting event was over, Bob Richards had won the Olympic championship for the second time with an Olympic record vault of 14 feet 11.5 inches—just one-half inch shy of his fifteen-foot goal.

It wasn't until some time later, while studying the films of his vaults, that Bob Richards discovered the reason why he could easily clear fifteen feet in practice, but not in competition. The films showed that when he tried to clear fifteen feet at the Olympic games, he did so with ease and with room to spare. But on his way down his hand went up and touched the crossbar just enough to jar it loose and make it tumble to the pit below. Through a subconscious act, he had actually caused his own failure!

Years later, Bob Richards told me that after giving it much thought and study, he realized why his subconscious was causing him to fail. It was because his early coaches had told him that he would never be a champion pole vaulter, especially a fifteen-foot vaulter—his legs were "too short." He anticipated failure!

Dr. Carl Rogers spent many years trying to find out why people succeed. What makes people such as Bruce Jenner, Wilma Rudolph, John Kennedy, James Michener, and scores of others like them winners? Dr. Rogers discovered an amazing secret: *winners are never surprised to win!* They *expect to win,* and not because they're self-centered, but because they have confidence in their training and abilities. If that's true, then *losers are never surprised to lose!*

That's why people fail. They expect to! In Job 3:25, Job says, "What I always feared has happened to me." He was looking for it; and when it came he wasn't surprised. When death, destruction, famine, plague, and disease all fell upon him and his family, he was saying, "I knew it." How many times have you said these words? How many times have we all said, "Oh, I knew that would happen"?

Dr. Will James was the first to identify this expectation of failure or success as the Law of Self-fulfilling Prophecy. "Be careful of what you expect because you're probably going to get it!" (We will discuss how this works in detail in chapter 4.)

PUTTING THE BLAME ON OTHERS

The second reason why people fail is that they blame others for their bad breaks in life. You might hear something such as, "The reason I haven't been successful in farming this year is because the government has put regulations on me and I have to plant crops I don't want to plant. The fertilizer company can't even make a decent fertilizer. It's never been this bad before. The bank won't give me the credit I need so I can buy new equipment. That's why I can't succeed."

Practically every president who ever served his country has blamed bad economic conditions, inflation, and the national debt on the previous administration. People in offices across the country complain, "I couldn't get my job done because Joe Smith in the next department didn't do his part." We almost never say, "I didn't succeed because I wasn't willing to do my part."

If we aren't blaming our peers or predecessors, we're blaming our leaders for holding us back and keeping us from being promoted so that we can have the success we want so desperately but aren't willing to work for.

If it isn't our leader's fault, then it certainly must be our spouse's fault. The wife nags too much and makes it impossible for the husband to concentrate and do his best. Or the husband just isn't a good provider and is always accusing the wife of spending too much money; or maybe he won't allow her to go out and get a job.

If it isn't the fault of our peers, leaders, or spouse, then it must be because of our handicaps. We have drawbacks and handicaps—age, race, creed, color, physical handicaps, etc. These limitations hold us back and prevent us from becoming all that we dream we can become.

(Yet, so many have surpassed overwhelming odds and handicaps to "become." Lord Byron and John Keats, two of the most respected poets of all time, had a clubbed foot and tuberculosis respectively. Gladstone became Prime Minister of Great Britain at the age of eighty; and J. P. Morgan didn't become a financial giant until after he was sixty years of age.)

If it isn't the fault of our peers, leaders, spouse, or our handicaps/drawbacks, then it must be God's fault. "God did this to me. I've done something to displease him somewhere in my past and now he's punishing me for it. Yes, it must be God's fault."

I once made eleven speeches in one week. Each time, without fail, someone would rush up to me after the speech to shake my hand and say, "I'm a self-made man," or "I'm a self-made woman." Not once did someone tell me, "I'm a self-made failure." Isn't it interesting that we're quick to take the credit for our successes, but also quick to immediately shift the blame to others when we fail?

When I'm home in Austin, Texas, I like to relax with the newspaper and catch up with what's been going on while I've been gone. The obituaries in the paper caught my eye one morning. They usually list the professions of the people who've died. That morning there were a banker, a mechanic, a homemaker, a teacher, a farmer, a taxi driver, and a doctor in the column.

On the following page I found the birth announcement column. As I read that list I didn't find that a banker, a mechanic, a homemaker, a teacher, a farmer, a taxi driver, and a doctor had been born—only babies. It dawned on me that it's not until we die that we become all we will ever be. And most of us never become anything because we're too busy blaming others for our mistakes, failures, and bad breaks in life.

SURRENDERING TO FEAR INSTEAD OF FAITH

Psychologists will agree that there are two basic drives in life: the will to live and the will to die. That's it. Everything else we do stems from these two basic drives. When we quit trying to live (faith), we begin trying to die (fear). It's that simple.

A baby is born with just two fears: the fear of falling and the fear of loud noises. That means that all other fears must be learned. People give in to those fears. It's a choice that's made, consciously or subconsciously.

Fear is the most destructive force in the world. Fear cripples motivation. Fear destroys enthusiasm. Fear will eventually rob you of love. Fear destroys all desire, all hope, all ambition, and promotes worry, doubt, feelings of inadequacy, and failure. Dr. Frank Minirth and Dr. Paul Meier tell us in their book, *Happiness Is a Choice,* that we find references throughout the Scriptures which indicate that fear is unhealthy (Philippians 4:6; 1 Peter 5:7). "There are approximately 350 passages in the Bible that tell us 'fear not.'"[1]

FEAR IS HOLDING MENTAL PICTURES OF WHAT YOU DON'T WANT TO HAPPEN

You begin to hold pictures in your mind of what you don't want to happen in your married life, your children's lives, your business, your social life, your spiritual life; and when those things do begin to happen, you're not surprised. You're right back to the anticipation of failure again. It becomes a vicious cycle which works on your mind and from which you have difficulty escaping.

I'm from Stamford, Texas, which on a busy Saturday has maybe three thousand people. I surprised everyone my senior year in high school by actually graduating from Stamford High School. After the graduation ceremony one of the teachers came over to talk to the seniors. Margaret Ann Crockett had taught my mother before me. She was sixty-four years old that year and was retiring from the teaching profession. She had decided to share something special with us, her last graduating class.

She said, "I'm going to give you that one thing that made my life worthwhile. Are you ready for it?"

"Yeah, Ma, we're ready," we all answered, calling her by that familiar name she'd grown to love.

"All right, here it is. . . . Whether you think you can or whether you think you can't, you're right!"

We all looked at each other with raised eyebrows and wondered if Ma had finally gone off the deep end. Then, we voted that what Ma Crockett had just stated was the dumbest thing ever said to seniors in the history of Stamford High School.

Twenty years later I discovered that Ma Crockett was a brilliant psychologist. She said to be careful of what you expect out of life because you're probably going to get it! That's the Law of Self-fulfilling Prophecy again. Don't anticipate failure, or you'll get it! Don't hold mental pictures of what you don't want to happen. Fear is a darkroom where negatives are developed. In order to be successful in life, a person must concentrate on the positives. Nothing can overcome fear except faith.

Faith is a difficult concept to describe. There have been

disagreements for centuries over the difference between belief and faith. The best example I've ever heard is that of a driver and a passenger in a car. The passenger gets into a car with a driver, *believing* that driver knows how to drive. Now that passenger can do one of two things. First, he can choose to stay alert, watching the traffic and lights, and telling the driver where to turn, etc. This passenger believes the driver can drive, but doesn't have much faith in his ability to do so.

The second thing the passenger can do is relax and fall asleep, letting the driver do the driving. Now, that's faith! Faith is a positive. *Faith is acting like it's so when it's not so in order for it to be so.* Remember what Rogers discovered in his study? Winners *expect* to win, therefore they *act* like winners. And so, they're never surprised when they win. That's powerful!

During the 1984 summer Olympics in Los Angeles, a small 4'9" American gymnast won the hearts of all Americans. Because of the performances of her and her teammates, America was on the verge of winning gold medals in women's gymnastics—a category so long dominated by the communist block countries.

Americans watched breathlessly as Mary Lou Retton readied herself for her final event, the vault—the event which would make or break her championship. She was a mere one-half point behind the first place gymnast. As she stood in the spotlight, with cameras turning and the crowd cheering, she concentrated on the vault before her. All of a sudden, as if the vault emitted a signal, she dipped her head in a quick, almost imperceptible nod, smiled, and then bounded down the path to complete her event. Mary Lou Retton scored a perfect 10! And then, to everyone's amazement, as if to prove that it wasn't a mistake, she took her second vault and scored another perfect 10!

What had she done? She had simply run the vault over in her mind, visualizing every perfect step. Then when she ran it, it came easily for her. Her coach had taught her *never to be surprised to win!*

Prior to those same Olympics, track and field athlete Carl

Lewis had announced the four events in which he would participate and the four gold medals which he would win. He was right in each case.

These two people *expected* to win. They concentrated on the positives. They held mental pictures of what they wanted to happen, not what they didn't want to happen.

After I spoke in California with Colonel Sanders, my friend Bob Richards and I went to see a young track star run the 100-yard dash. He hit the tape in 9.1 seconds. The crowd loved him. They cheered and shouted and were ecstatic when he finished with a record time. Afterward, Bob and I rushed to the track to talk with him.

Bob asked him to remove his left shoe. The young athlete bent down, untied and took off his left shoe. He then removed a neatly folded piece of paper. As he slowly unfolded it, I could see "9.1" scrawled across it.

Fear is acting in accord with what you don't want to happen. Faith is acting in accord with what you *do* want to happen.

NO GOALS

After I spoke to the realtors in California and just before Colonel Sanders spoke, former New York Yankees catcher Yogi Berra entered the room. The host asked him to say a few words. I should mention that Yogi Berra was a great catcher, but he isn't known as a good speaker. However, that day he said something that impressed me even though I couldn't understand him.

Yogi Berra said, "If you don't know where you're going in life, you're liable to wind up somewhere else!"

That sounded profound, so I wrote it down. During my ride back to the airport I tried to figure out what it meant. Finally it came to me. He meant if you don't know where you're going, how will you ever know when you get there? Do you know where you'll be five years from now, or even where you'd like to be? Do you know where you're headed in life? If you're like 90 percent of the rest of Americans, you don't know.

In 1865, Lewis Carroll wrote a fabulous children's classic, *Alice's Adventures in Wonderland*. After chasing a rabbit down a rabbit hole, young Alice meets all sorts of strange creatures in a weird, upside-down world. On her journey through this adventure, she soon spies the grinning Cheshire Cat sitting on a bough in a tree beside the road.

"Would you tell me, please, which way I ought to go from here?"

"That depends a good deal on where you want to get to," said the Cat.

"I don't much care where—," said Alice.

"Then it doesn't matter which way you go," said the Cat.

"—so long as I get *somewhere*," Alice added as an explanation.

"Oh, you're sure to do that," said the Cat.[2]

The fourth reason why people fail is that they have no clear-cut, written, specific, definable, achievable, believable goals for their lives. People spend more time planning vacations than they do planning their lives. Aim at nothing and you'll hit it every time!

The latest studies show that the average life span after retirement is three years unless the retiree has a regular hobby or second vocation. Helen Hayes, a lovely accomplished actress, was interviewed on television in early 1984. After nearly sixty years in show business, her doctors told her she must retire because of her continuous struggle with asthma. Since retiring from TV and films, except for occasional brief guest appearances, she has had a successful radio call-in show for women.

When asked why she continued to work after so many years, she answered, "A person must have a goal to work toward. Otherwise, there's nothing to live for."

People by nature are goal-seeking, goal-striving beings. Without goals they drift aimlessly. Without purpose they go nowhere, ultimately feeling like worthless, useless human beings. People need goals to function effectively. Otherwise, especially after retirement, they often find they have no reason for living. Illness may follow, with some eventually dying a premature death. People without goals become frustrated, hypochondriacal, unhappy, depressed, and embittered. They begin to drift into a state of mediocrity, filling psychologists' offices all over the country.

The mere setting of goals helps you develop direction. As you see those goals accomplished, your self-confidence and self-worth continue to grow. We're like bicycles, which stand upright as long as we have forward motion toward a goal. But we, like bicycles, fall when we no longer have direction in our lives.

While in New York for a speech several years ago, my host invited me to see a Broadway play. Now, I must confess, we have very few Broadway plays in Stamford, Texas. I was excited just to see a Broadway theater from the outside, not to mention an actual play. So naturally, I accepted my host's gracious invitation.

He picked me up at my hotel and took me out to dinner. Then we went to see *Death of a Salesman*. I found it to be a miserable play—discouraging, depressing, and demeaning.

The main character in *Death of a Salesman* is Willy Loman—a sixty-four-year-old salesman who, after thirty-four years of failure, dies poverty stricken. I became depressed early on, not wanting to sit through the entire show. But, as someone's guest, and as a conspicuous occupant of a front row seat, I had no choice. All through the first two acts, I sat there trying to think up excuses to get out of that theater.

Finally, the third act curtain went up. It was then that I really saw *Death of a Salesman*. Then the play seemed to come together and finally make some sense. It is at this point that Willy Loman dies. His wife and sons gather around his grave to say their last good-bye's.

"He had the wrong dreams," one son says. "The man didn't know who he was."[3]

ANATOMY OF A FAILURE

I believe Arthur Miller wrote *Death of a Salesman* in order to say that a major cause of failure is when people have no goals for their lives—something that can help them through the trouble spots, the difficulties, the pressures of life. Every great person who ever lived was, at one time, an unknown, seemingly nonexistent. That is, until he set a goal for his life. John Rockefeller was a bookkeeper making twenty-five dollars a month. It was his goals which drove him to become the master of an oil dynasty. Henry Ford was a bicycle mechanic until his goals urged him to become the king of an automobile empire.

A young teenage girl once dreamed of becoming a great writer. (She completed her first novel at age sixteen.) Everyone laughed and made fun of her, telling her she was just being foolish. They laughed at her so much that she gave up her dreams and tried to commit suicide. She spent the next twenty years of her life in utter misery, working as a nurse and a maid. But twenty years after her first unsuccessful attempt, her dreams urged her to seek her lifetime goal. Louisa Mae Alcott wrote *Little Women* and proved to the world, including those who laughed at her, that she could do well the thing she loved most.

Vince Lombardi, the late and great head coach of the Green Bay Packers football team, was an assistant line coach at Fordham University at age forty-five. Bob Devaney, the number one winning coach in college football while at Nebraska, was an assistant high school coach at Michigan at age forty-five.

I once shared a program with a man who is supposed to be the greatest basketball coach of all time. He's the only man to be placed in the Basketball Hall of Fame as both a player and a coach. John Wooden stood in front of six thousand people and told them that he didn't have a winning season during the first thirteen years he coached. He was fifty-one years old before he had a winning season. During the next thirteen years his UCLA basketball teams won *ten* national championships!

Someone in the audience asked, "John, what's your secret?"

"I get a goal I can work toward," he answered. "It lifts me,

41

it guides me, and it gives me direction."

I know. You're probably thinking that these people are exceptions, not like most people. But they really were like anybody else until they got a goal to work toward and strive for. Harlan Sanders was a sixty-five-year-old retired cook, Henry Ford a bicycle mechanic, Wilma Rudolph a crippled teenager, Bob Devaney a high school football coach, John Rockefeller a bookkeeper, and Abraham Lincoln an unknown, self-educated country lawyer. And they all *made it!* They became all that they had ever dreamed of becoming.

In 1983 I traveled to Seattle where I met a young lady who shared the program with me. She and her husband were in the grocery business, and after about eleven years it began to fail. They both went out and got second jobs selling vitamins in order to try to make ends meet and support their family.

Her husband couldn't make enough money selling vitamins, so he got a job in a nearby logging camp instead. Within three weeks' time he'd broken his back and was lying in a hospital bed, no longer able to provide for his family.

They decided that the grocery store just wasn't going to survive without him. So, they declared bankruptcy, and she began teaching sewing classes in addition to selling vitamins. These two incomes helped keep food on the table until her husband recovered from his accident and began looking for a new job. Things were looking up and going along pretty well for a change.

Then, just as suddenly as her husband had been struck down, she was involved in a tragic car accident which left *her* lying on her back in a hospital bed for the next five years of her life. It's at that point that most people would simply give up and live on welfare for the rest of their lives. But, this young woman continued to teach her sewing classes from her bed while her family somehow managed to run their home without her.

It was while lying in that bed that she developed a new sewing technique. Excited about this new discovery, her husband encouraged and supported her. In the evenings after the children were in bed, he would bring rolls of butcher paper to her bedside. Together they would stay up into the morning hours cutting out patterns for her classes the next day.

Today, her sewing technique is taught across the country and nets her several million dollars annually. Many women have taken classes in "Stretch & Sew"—a relatively new technique developed by Ann Person in a lonely hospital bed. How did she do that?

Ann Person wanted to become more than she was. She had incredible odds to overcome—a failed business, an injured husband, a personally devastating injury, and a family to feed and clothe. But she didn't anticipate failure. When she had to work two jobs to make ends meet after her husband's accident, and when she herself met with tragedy, she didn't put the blame on others. She didn't surrender to fear and carry around mental pictures of what she didn't want to happen. Just the opposite. She concentrated on the positives and was able to set goals to work toward—goals which resulted in a new sewing technique which has revolutionized the sewing industry and made an impact on the design of sewing equipment itself.

You, too, can be the person you want to be, were created to be, and have the right to be. *Anyone can be a winner!*

PART TWO
THE SECOND GREATEST STORY EVER TOLD

3
POTENTIAL vs. PERFORMANCE

THE OLD MAN stood rooted to the rocky soil in shocked disbelief; his long white beard flowing in the warm breeze, his gnarled hands grasping his shepherd's staff. He was eighty years old, having been a shepherd for forty years. He had a speech impediment, and now he was being asked to lead millions.

"Impossible!" he protested.

The shepherd gave not one, but *five* reasons why he couldn't do it: (1) He wasn't the person for the job. (2) He was afraid that people wouldn't understand who had sent him. (3) He was afraid that people wouldn't believe him. (4) He felt he wasn't a good enough speaker to be a leader. And finally, (5) he wanted someone else to be sent in his place. Anticipating resistance and rejection from his people, Moses felt that God was using poor judgment in selecting him for such a significant task (cf. Exodus 3-4).

If Moses were living today, he would be labeled a failure.

He'd murdered an Egyptian and fled into the desert to live the following forty years of his life as a shepherd. All the education which he'd received at the Pharaoh's palace could do him no good there. His self-image, the picture in his mind of what he believed himself to be, was so poor that he had the nerve to stand up and argue with his Creator about his abilities. Nevertheless, God, knowing Moses' potential, selected him—an eighty-year-old shepherd and murderer—to lead millions of captive Israelites out of Egyptian bondage in the greatest mass exodus of all time.

Everyone, at some time in life, will feel as inadequate as Moses felt, unworthy of the task before her—"Who, me?" This is normal. However, when a persons feels this way most or all of the time, it's often the result of poor self-esteem. A person's self-image, how she views herself as a person, determines her attitudes toward life situations which she'll confront on a daily basis.

The best preparation for success is to have a strong, healthy self-image. It's the very core of your personality, affecting every aspect of your behavior. It controls your ability to learn, your rate of growth and change, and the choices you make with respect to friends, career, and a mate. The self-image you have is your source for personal happiness. It establishes the boundaries of your accomplishments. It defines the limits of your fulfillment. Your self-image is your opinion of who you are divided by your opinion of what it takes to do your job. The result is the way you behave throughout your lifetime.

With so much failure surrounding us, how can we establish healthy self-images and view ourselves as winners? A study conducted in Palo Alto, California, revealed that there are several things a person must do to have the kind of life, business, career, and success he wants to have. There are several ways in which a person must act if he is going to become the person he dreams of becoming. (These will be discussed in detail throughout the remaining chapters of this book.)

SEE YOURSELF AS A WINNER

The number one thing you must do to become a winner is *believe* that you have the right to be successful. A winner isn't blessed with unusual abilities over and above the norm; say, for example, a person who has an unusually high IQ. (As a matter of fact, experts tell us that most of us never develop over 7 percent of our intelligence potential anyway.) Nor is a winner someone who has been singled out by God as special. A winner is simply a man or a woman who sees the possibility of becoming successful and does what it takes to achieve it. And a winner does it *without hurting others or compromising her beliefs and convictions.*

School teachers once told a young sixteen-year-old that he should give up and quit school. They told him he would never be successful because he wasn't smart enough. In fact, most of his teachers all through school had told him that he would never amount to anything worthwhile. They told him the only work he would ever be able to do was manual labor.

Between the ages of sixteen and thirty-two he'd held sixty-seven different jobs. He'd drifted from one job to another, unable to be successful at any of them. For some reason, at age thirty-two he was given an IQ test. The people who administered the test were shocked to learn that he had an IQ of 161!

Today that man is a well-known scientist, working with lasers and other modern scientific inventions. He was even president of the Mensa Society for two years—an organization which requires an IQ of 145 for membership.

At age thirty-two he was considered an idiot. At age thirty-three he was recognized as a genius, studying to make up for all the education he'd missed. How could he make such a dramatic change within only a few months? How could a supposed idiot become one of the world's leading scientists? Because he was able to change the way he *saw himself.* The secret to being a winner is to see yourself as a winner and *believe* that you can make it. People actually perform the way they see themselves performing in their minds.

I once spoke at Tulane University in New Orleans. After

my speech, a young man rushed from the back of the room. He grabbed my hand and started pumping it up and down. I thought, "Oh, boy, he really loved my speech!"

"I want to meet you and shake your hand because you're a fraud," he said.

Now that got my attention! I hadn't been called a fraud in a while, and I thought it was an interesting way to start a conversation.

"Why do you think I'm a fraud?" I asked.

"Because you go around saying people can change what they are and that just isn't true. I'm a scientist, and it's been proved scientifically that you're a product of your heredity and environment and that's it. People are born into a mold into which they stay for the rest of their lives. You just can't change what you are."

Another speaker on the program stood behind me, listening to this young professor express his beliefs. He looked over my shoulder at the scientist and asked, "Sir, would you become involved in a program with me to see if Lewis is a fraud or not?"

"What?" he asked incredulously.

"I'm going to be here for a few months. Would you become involved in a scientific experiment to find out if Lewis is a fraud? Is he for real or not? Does his advice have any validity? Now, if we're wrong, we'll apologize to you. But if we're right, you simply apologize to us."

"I'm a scientist," he responded. "I'll be glad to do it as long as the experiment in conducted scientifically. What do you want me to do?"

The following morning, they met at the personnel office at Tulane University. There they asked the personnel director for the name of a university employee who'd been labeled a "loser." They wanted a man or a woman who would never be able to achieve or progress beyond his or her present status in life.

After going through the files, the personnel director found two men, both janitors. They administered a series of psychological and academic tests to these two men and found that one of them couldn't even be taught to type—definitely a "loser." They said he would always be a janitor—that because he had no education, no background experience, and poor job performance, he could never be successful.

My two friends took this young janitor and shared with him what I'm sharing with you throughout this book. Days turned into weeks, weeks into months, and months into years as he put into practice all that he'd learned.

If you should go to Tulane University today and ask for that same janitor, you wouldn't find him. The young man who couldn't be taught to type went on to become the head computer programmer for a life insurance company in New Orleans, making more than $25,000 a year. If you met him today, you'd meet a proud, educated man who likes himself and knows he's a winner.

Today, many businesses show a film of this young man's miraculous achievement in order to demonstrate to their employees that if they can just get into their mind's eye the truth—that they were created to be the best they can be—then they can accomplish great things, too. That janitor finally came to know that he counted in this world. He finally came to realize that he's somebody special. Your self-image has *nothing* whatsoever to do with your potential, but *everything* to do with your performance.

Dr. Dorothy Jongeward, author of *Everybody Wins,* has said that we're born to win and conditioned to lose. Something or someone begins to tear down that picture of what you want to be. You allow it to reduce you, step by step, to the point where you accept less than the best for yourself. It's in this condition that most of us pass through life, believing that we can never do better or be better than what we are now.

In Matthew 22:39, we are commanded to love our neighbors as (we love) ourselves. This tells me that before people can respond positively and effectively with love toward others, they must first love themselves. We were created to love who we are, not to live up to someone else's standards and expectations. To be successful, to be what you want to be, you've got to see yourself as a winner and develop a positive, healthy self-image.

UNDERSTAND BEHAVIOR SOURCES

I said earlier that the self-image is the very core of a person's personality, affecting every aspect of behavior. There's a definite connection between the self-image in the subconscious and the ultimate behavior resulting from it. This can be seen as a process.

To begin with, the self-image controls a person's attitudes, or interpretations of what happens to her, based on what she believes herself to be. A person's basic attitudes will give you a clue as to whether that person likes herself or not. There are those who will get up in the morning and say, "Good morning, Lord." And then there are those who will get up and say, "Good Lord, it's morning." Which kind are you?

Many of us have heard parents and teachers tell children, or bosses tell employees, that they must change their attitudes. I can hear a good speech or a great sermon and get all excited and tell myself I'm going to change my attitude and do great things; and then something goes wrong. You know the process. The minute something goes wrong, my attitude goes back into my subconscious and checks with my self-image. It tells me, "Don't kid me, Lewis, you're from Stamford, Texas. You have never been a winner. What makes you think you can be one now? Are you kidding me?"

It's impossible to change a person's attitudes without first changing that person's self-image—the source of those attitudes. (You will learn how to do this in succeeding chapters.)

The self-image controls your attitudes, which in turn control your needs. A person with a positive, healthy self-image who sets goals to strive toward will have different needs than a person with low self-esteem who is starving for affection and is apathetic toward goals because he can never see himself as successful. Drives and motivation come from this basic chain. This is what moves us to become what we want to be. This is where fear and faith are located. You must begin with a healthy self-image if you're going to fulfill your needs; if you're going to have the things necessary to survive, and then be successful in life. This, in turn, presents positive attitudes and the motivation and drive to set goals.

The motivation and desire that push people such as Ann Person to succeed come as a result of a decision deep down inside that you have a right to performance, promise, position, and most importantly, personhood. You have a right to be successful, and the things that are holding you back are deep within you. The secret to success begins in the subconscious mind with a strong self-image. Such a view of oneself takes years to develop, but can be positively changed with a little work.

Successful people are willing to set goals and pay the necessary price for success and accomplishment. Why won't people do what it takes to be successful? Ann Person was a victim of circumstance, of near failure; yet she turned her life into something positive while others might have given up. Why? What pushes the few to pay the price and do the things that unsuccessful people won't do? The answer to that question lies in a good self-image which provides people with the necessary attitudes and motivation.

The self-image controls your attitudes which control your needs which, in turn, control your emotions. From your emotions come your habit patterns. We live the majority of our lives by habit. Let's try an experiment.

Hold your hands out in front of you and clasp them together, intertwining your fingers as if you're going to pray. Notice which thumb rests on top, the right or the left. Now release your hands and clasp them together again, only this time put the other thumb on top. You had a problem, didn't you? You can try the same experiment by crossing your arms. We're creatures of habit.

Habits come from the subconscious mind. Maltz writes, "If your habits are wholesome, you *must be* a happy person. If they are not, you should make every effort to change them—so that you can live a fuller, more vivacious life."[1]

Your habits are an important part of your life. You need them to function. Fortunately, habits are automatic. Imagine the person who hasn't acquired good hygiene habits going off to work in the mornings without a shower, without brushing his teeth, and without combing his hair.

All of our habits reflect subconscious feelings or emotions. Psychologists believe that people with bad habits have negative emotions or feelings about themselves—in other words, low self-esteem. But Maltz says that ". . . habits can be good, even inspiring, and the whole art of living is to overcome bad habits and rise above them to habits that make for a good life."[2]

A person's emotions control her ultimate behavior. We've now touched the end of the chain. Your self-image controls your attitudes. If, because of your life-style, background, status, past experiences, or physical appearance, you don't believe yourself to be a winner, you'll begin to look for a reason or an excuse to fail. That, in turn, will affect your attitude, which will affect those things you need in life, which will affect your basic emotions and habit patterns, which will affect your ultimate behavior. Thus, you'll see yourself as a loser. You'll start acting like a loser, destined to fail. And then, you won't be surprised when you do. Failure is a direct result of poor self-esteem and the anticipation of failure. Your ultimate behavior takes the chain full circle because it's a direct reflection of your self-image.

There's a young lady from the midwest whom I greatly admire. In 1983, she was ranked the third best high diver in her state, only 2.5 points behind the first place diver. Today she's preparing herself to become a world champion high diver.

Recently, she was honored with an award for typing forty-three words per minute. Most typists know that forty-three words per minute is no great accomplishment for a typist; but my young friend has no arms! She types with her toes and dives with no arms. In spite of a serious disabling handicap, she sees herself as a winner and believes in herself. Her attitudes and behavior reflect that belief and positive self-image. It's because of this belief in herself that she's able to surpass overwhelming odds and accomplish great things.

Your self-image is everything you've ever learned or been told about yourself, whether it's true or not. You can do great things if you'll only believe that you can. Your self-image has everything to do with your behavior, your performance, your reactions to situations, and the events around you. However, your self-image has nothing whatsoever to do with your potential—what you have the ability to become as a person and accomplish in your lifetime. *Anyone can be a winner!*

54

4

A WONDERFUL, POWERFUL, AND AWESOME THING

OBEDIENTLY FOLLOWING HIS teacher's instructions, the little nine-year-old boy went to the blackboard and began drawing a picture for that day's art lesson. He tried to draw the best picture he'd ever drawn. When he was finished he stood back and proudly admired his work. He called his teacher over to show her his masterpiece, and when she looked at it she laughed. Her laughter rang through the silent classroom, providing a signal to the class. Before long, everyone was laughing. The small nine-year-old boy rushed out into the hall in embarrassment and tears.

Running blindly down the corridor, he bumped into his sister. She asked him why he was crying. He proceeded to tell her the whole story; a story that would remain embedded deep within his subconscious mind.

Years later, when this young man was attending the University of Texas, one of his art professors discovered that he had a tremendous talent for art. But each time the professor tried to get him to draw, he would just give up and quit.

You see, when our little friend first told his sister what had happened, it was the second time it had happened as far as his subconscious was concerned. When he told his best friend after school, his mind received this experience for the third time. Later, he went home and told his mother—a fourth time. Then he told his father when he came home from work—a fifth time. In a period of three hours he'd relived that scene of embarrassment, of crying, of knowing that if he drew a picture people would laugh at him, five times. And from that point on, he decided never to draw again.

His wise professor, having seen the flashes of genius, called a psychologist friend and asked for help. The psychologist took this young student through hypnotherapy, slowly walking him back, step by step, to his fourth-grade classroom. It was there that he uncovered the reason for the boy's hesitation to draw.

Through continued therapy, the young man began to realize that what had happened to him ten years earlier was the result of his teacher's opinions and unrealistic expectations of perfection, and that these opinions and expectations weren't based on fact. He began to see that he'd been living his life based on someone else's critical opinion of him, not on his own talents and abilities. By reliving it over and over each time he told the story, and each time he sat down in art class to draw, he was reinforcing the negative programming that had been planted in his mind when he was only nine years old.

Shortly after this life-changing realization, he won the outstanding art student's award at the University of Texas. This couldn't have been achieved had he not been given help in realizing that he'd lived ten years of his life believing himself an artistic failure, believing that if he drew anything at all people would laugh at him. You don't have to have a lifetime history of failure to decide that you are a failure. You only need one bad experience reinforced a number of times. Your subconscious mind can't tell the difference between a real or an imagined experience. Every time you vividly recreate the same scene in your mind, your mind thinks it's happening again in reality. Your subconscious begins to accept you as a failure; not because it's true, but because *you believe* it's true, and because you keep going over it in your mind again and again.

Our self-image is acquired through years of experiences, successes, and failures, and is reinforced each time we succeed or fail again. It is formed from earliest childhood and is affected by how we see others viewing us, by what we think others expect of us, by what we imagine society expects of us, and by our relationships with others, including God.

Recent scientific studies reveal that babies respond to moods, thoughts, emotions, etc., from the sixth month of pregnancy on. The mental tape recorders are running with infants, developing their subconscious thought patterns before birth. Babies arrive in this world subconsciously knowing that they're wanted, loved, and worthwhile, or, that they're unwanted, unloved, and not worthwhile. Those feelings and thoughts begin to manifest themselves in the behavior of children. Everything is stored for the whole life in the subconscious, and by the time a child is six years old, the self-image is practically set.

John Stossel, reporter for ABC TV's "20/20," reported in April of 1984 that psychiatrists now use psychotherapy on babies in their first year of life. Most babies needing such therapy have been emotionally deprived of eye contact, touching, loving, soothing, and caressing—the very things essential to good emotional well-being. These latest studies have revealed that it's impossible to "spoil" a baby during its first year—a time when these emotional contacts are so critical to its development. Children who have received the most attention during the first year of life have grown up to be the most loving and least demanding. They also have the most positive and healthy self-images.

Most of us go through life never understanding ourselves or why we act the way we do. Few people, including scientists, understand how the mind works. The mind is a wonderful, powerful, and awesome thing. If we wanted to mechanically duplicate its functions, hidden in the deep recesses of a small three-pound brain, we would need a building as tall as the Empire State Building in New York City and as long as the Cow Palace in San Francisco. That's mind-boggling in and of itself!

THE CONSCIOUS MIND

The mind is divided into two parts: the conscious and the subconscious. It's like an iceberg floating on the ocean's surface. The small tip, visible above the surface, represents the conscious mind, the part of our mind which acts like a computer. This part has four basic functions.

1. The conscious mind *receives* all information. Everything you've ever learned comes through the conscious mind. It deals with facts. It receives information based on what you hear, taste, touch, smell, and see. You learn through this part of your mind—the part which houses your reasoning power or logic.

2. The conscious mind *associates* everything you learn with past events and experiences. The second anything comes into your mind through your various senses, it goes back and checks the data bank of the past and asks, "Has this happened to me before? Do I like this? Do I hate this? Do I enjoy this or not? What did I do the last time this happened?"

Once, while speaking at a convention, I had the opportunity to eat at a lavish banquet which had been prepared for the conventioneers. The waiter brought out a strange-looking green appetizer with something wrapped up inside it.

One of the men at my table opened his up, ate it, and remarked, "This is fantastic! I've never tasted anything so delicious. I love it!"

He called the waiter over to our table and told him he must compliment the chef on the delicious appetizer that he'd just eaten. The waiter disappeared into the kitchen and returned with the chef.

"I must have the recipe," my friend exclaimed. "This is fabulous. What's in it?"

"Thank you very much," the chef responded. "That's made of spinach, mushrooms, and cheese."

My friend almost had a heart attack right on the spot! He

refused to eat another bite of that "delicious" appetizer. He didn't like spinach! In fact, he *hated* spinach; so much so that it made him sick whenever he ate it. He thought that no one in his right mind would ever even look at spinach, much less eat it. But, he had loved the delicacy until he learned what was in it.

3. His mind went back into its memory bank, checked with past events, and said, "Hey, wait a minute. You don't like spinach, so you can't eat that." The conscious mind *evaluates* the information it finds. It goes back and checks with the past before it lets you know whether you should or should not proceed.

4. Finally, the conscious mind *acts,* making a decision based on what it has learned from the memory bank. Each time the young art student sat down to draw, his mind told him, "You can't draw. In fact, you draw so badly that people laugh at you. So you won't draw anymore." The decision to act (or not to act) comes from the evaluation and association that the mind has already performed for you. Where are the things the mind checks and associates with? In the subconscious mind.

THE SUBCONSCIOUS MIND

Experts tell us that we may have as many as fifteen billion neurons in each of our brains, yet we use only 6 or 7 percent of them. Einstein used only around 22 percent of his brain power. People have so much untapped potential. But the subconscious mind, and thus the self-image, is like the remainder of the iceberg, floating deep beneath the surface of the water, its massive bulk hidden from view. All our experiences and thoughts are stored here permanently; and though it's out of sight, it affects the conscious mind, the way we behave and react to situations, and every decision we make during our lifetimes.

Like the conscious, the subconscious mind has four basic functions.

1. The subconscious *stores* all information. Everything you've ever heard, read, seen, thought, or been told is stored

in your subconscious. Before you're thirty years old, you'll have three trillion memories in your subconscious. You never forget a thing except *how* to recall all that you know.

To illustrate, let's try another experiment. Complete the following statements:

    a. Winston tastes good like ....[1]
    b. Pepsi Cola hits..[2]
    c. Lucky Strike means ....[3]

These three ads last ran approximately fifteen years ago. If you are at least twenty-five years old, all you probably needed to remember them was a gentle reminder from the past. I'm sure you haven't used these phrases lately, yet they probably popped out of your subconscious storehouse at the push of your memory button. We're memory-oriented and do things because our subconscious remembers the first time we did them and tells us how to do them again.

When a baby first reaches for its rattle, its motions are jerky and unstable. All the while, its mental computer is making corrections. Eventually, it reaches out and grasps the toy with its chubby little hand. From that moment on, its subconscious mind has registered how reaching and grasping are to be done. And each time the baby tries, the task becomes a little easier to accomplish. The subconscious mind works the same for all of us, storing information for future reference.

A number of years ago, I was asked by a large bank in California to teach its executives how to become salesmen. Times were getting pretty tough economically, and competition between various banks and savings and loan companies was fierce. Their people were having to go out and make sales calls to bring in business. Now most people don't become bankers in order to go out and make sales calls. These people thought such work was beneath them, and I could tell they were really unhappy about the whole idea.

After the first session, the senior vice-president came up to me and asked if we could talk for a few minutes. I could tell he was really uncomfortable and extremely upset.

"I like you real well," he began. "But I want you to know

that I'm not coming back to this class."

"I can tell you like me a lot," I responded. I then asked him why he was leaving the class if he really did like what I was doing.

"No, no, it's not you," he said. "It's just that I'm not going to be any ———, ———, ——— salesman! I'm fifty-four years old, and I didn't go into banking to become a salesman. No one likes a salesman. Salesmen are the scum of the earth. People spit on salesmen and slam doors in their faces. I wouldn't be a salesman if I were starving!"

"Tell me about the first time you were a salesman," I asked him.

He looked as though I'd shot him right between the eyes. Startled by my remark, he asked, "How could you tell?"

"Well, that's pretty obvious," I answered.

Then he began relating his story. When he was nineteen years old and in college, he got a job as a Bible salesman in order to pay his college expenses. He went door to door selling Bibles. Now, you and I know how some people can treat door-to-door salesmen. People told him just what they thought of him, described his ancestry in "glowing" terms, and told him in no uncertain language what he could do with his Bibles. They slammed doors in his face, chewed him up, and spit him out. No wonder he decided that selling was a scum-of-the-earth business.

Now, at age fifty-four, and as senior vice-president of his bank, he was being asked to return to selling in order to help the bank through tough economic times. The first memories that came to him when his boss asked him to attend my class were those experiences at age nineteen. His mind went back into its memory bank and told him, "Hey, wait a minute! I remember when I was nineteen. That's a lousy, stinking, thankless life. I won't do that again. It's bad for me. It makes me feel terrible. It hurts. I won't do it."

He made a decision based on the associations and evaluations that his mind made with past experiences. Even if it meant losing his job, he would quit the salesmanship class. He would rather be penniless and starving than be a salesman again.

What happens to you if, as an adult, you've gone through

61

life storing up impressions about yourself that you're bad, that you're not going to be successful in life, that you've always been poor, and that you've always been incapable in many ways? What's going to happen when you find you have a great opportunity to be somebody or to do something wonderful for others, and your mind goes back and checks with those past experiences in its memory bank? You're going to say, "I can't do that. I'm not educated enough. I've never been capable of anything like that." That will be your self-image talking to you, perhaps causing you to miss the opportunity of a lifetime.

Your self-image isn't based on truth. It develops based on what you *believe* to be true. The conscious mind deals with facts and truth, but it has to go back to both truths and untruths in your subconscious in order to associate and evaluate information. The subconscious has no critical judgment with which to discern the difference. It will accept anything you tell it, whether it's negative or positive, true or untrue; and it will work to achieve any goal you set for it.

> People under hypnosis have taken action on the most unlikely truths. Told that water is champagne, they have become intoxicated. Informed that the weather is warm, they have perspired; then told that it is cold (same situation, same temperature), they have shivered and put on additional clothing. . . . These people, under hypnosis, accepted new truths—some false, some true. . . . How about yourself? What is the truth about yourself?[4]

Your subconscious is like soil that accepts any seed, good or bad, and then proceeds to grow what has been planted. Negative, destructive points of view will work through the subconscious to ensure that you have negative, destructive experiences. Constructive points of view can grow into prosperous, confidence-building, positive experiences—just as surely as an acorn grows, not into poison ivy, but a giant oak.

Our minds must absorb thousands of thoughts, pieces of information, etc., every second of every day. We don't want or need much of it, so the mind also acts as a filter to that information it receives. There are things in the mind known as scotomas, or "blind spots," which filter out unwanted or useless information. The only problem is that the subconscious can arbitrarily filter out truth as well as falsehood. After this filtering process is complete, we begin to see things as we *want* to see them. We see what we want to believe is true and then act upon it as truth.

For example, in the following sentence you're going to find two or three *fs*. Some people find three *fs*, but most people only find two. Now, count the number of *fs* you see in this sentence.

Finished files are the result of years of scientific study combined with the experience of many years.

How many *fs* did you find? Two? Three? There are *six!* Now, I have to admit that I set you up by telling you that you'd only *find* two or three. So, your mind probably believed that only three were there. I didn't say there were only three. But if you're in the majority, that's what you believed.

Count how many times the word "of" appears. It appears three times; but we pronounce "of" as "ov." And the subconscious mind picks it up as "ov." We don't see it as "of" with our eyes. That's the scotoma working. We say "ov," so we see "ov" subconsciously.

In other words, if someone says, "You're never going to be successful; I don't think you'll ever amount to anything in life," you'll eventually begin to look for truth to reinforce that person's opinion. If you don't *see* your potential in your subconscious, it may as well not be there at all.

My friend mentioned in chapter 3 lost sixty-seven jobs and believed himself to be an idiot until someone convinced him he was a genius. It wasn't until then that he was able to see his true potential and tap into his reservoir to make something of his life. Your mind can actually go to work to prove that you're right about yourself, even when you're not.

Dr. Eric Berne says in his book, *Games People Play,* that the only time some of us feel good about ourselves is when we are right about how wrong we are. Isn't that terrible?

That means that some of us only feel good about ourselves when we can prove to others that we're not successful. The scotoma in your mind directs you to act not upon truth, but upon *perceived* truth; and all in an effort to resist change.

In 1975, the city government in one of this country's largest cities spent $47 million to turn a run-down, dilapidated slum into a beautiful housing project for its residents. In less than one year after its completion, this magnificent project had been turned back into a broken-down slum. City officials brought in behavioral specialists to determine why this tragedy had occurred. After surveys and interviews with the project's residents, the specialists said the most common remark was, "We don't deserve homes like this."

As mentioned earlier, Maltz says every person is born with the right to be successful, but that we accept less and less as our standard for success until we finally settle for mediocrity. In a related sense, we love to operate within a "climate zone," an area of our lives where we feel comfortable. We begin to feel so comfortable that our subconscious mind acts like a thermostat, making strong efforts to keep us in a state of "no change."

A few years ago, a company called me to train about sixteen thousand of their salesmen. About a year before the program was to begin, I sent a psychologist ahead to do some surveys and testing for me. One of the things this psychologist did was take the two salesmen in this company who were at the very top and the very bottom in sales and reverse their territories.

We took Salesman A, who had averaged $50,000 a year for seven consecutive years, and transferred him to a territory previously held by Salesman B, who'd only earned $11,000 a year for seven years. Salesman B was placed in the territory which had yielded $50,000 a year in revenue.

Guess how much money Salesman A, who used to earn $50,000 a year, made in his new territory that had averaged $11,000 a year? $50,000! How much money do you think Salesman B, who used to make $11,000 a year, made in the territory which had averaged $50,000 a year? $11,000! Why?

When our psychologist asked Salesman B why he made only one-fourth of his new territory's potential income, he responded, "Because I'm an $11,000 a year guy!"

He'd reached his comfort, or climate, zone. His self-image told him, "Whoa!" every time he reached $11,000. He couldn't see himself making more money, so his subconscious worked to ensure that he stayed there. He felt that $11,000 was all he was worth, all that he was capable of earning.

Then we decided to sandbag him. We set up a big sale for the third month of the second year. Remember, he'd been averaging $11,000 a year, about $916 a month. For the first two months he made a little over $1,000. During the third month he made the sale which we'd set up. He made $4,000 commission that month alone. Now he was ahead financially and had the potential to make more than his average of $916 per month.

How much did he make the fourth month following this set-up? *Nothing!* He planned to go to work each day, and sometimes he did. But he didn't make one sale all month because he'd exceeded his comfort zone. He had some extra money to get him by now. He made nothing again the fifth month! It took him four months to get back to his old pattern; and when he did go back to work seriously, he made $900 per month. At the end of the year—you guessed it—he had made exactly $11,000!

All of us see ourselves, in varying degrees, as a plus or a minus. Somewhere along the scale, we'll find our comfort zone and behave in ways that will keep us there. Our self-image in our subconscious will work like a thermostat, constantly working to keep the environment around it as close as possible to the standard that has been set for it. Your comfort zone, whatever it may be, is a direct reflection of your self-image.

Do you do poor or average work at your job to avoid a promotion because you don't think you deserve to be in a better position? Or might it be because you think you won't be capable of doing work at a higher level? Did you make bad or barely passing grades in school because you felt, or had been told, that you weren't as smart as your friends or the brothers and sisters who had gone before you? If so, you've worked to stay in a comfort zone created by what others have told you and expected of you along the way during your lifetime; and you probably didn't even realize what was happening. Your mind has kept you in your comfort zone because of what you *believed* to be true, not due to actual truth.

2. Besides storing all information, both true and untrue, the subconscious mind *acts* as a problem-solving mechanism. The conscious mind can call upon the power and resources of the subconscious, and it will work to solve any problem desired by an individual. The subconscious never sleeps. It works twenty-four hours a day, many times solving a problem long after it's been abandoned by the conscious.

Most of us have either experienced, or heard of, instances in which a problem seemed impossible to solve prior to going to bed; yet, after a night's sleep, the answer became clear in the morning when the subconscious reintroduced it to the conscious mind.

Or, perhaps you've had a name "on the tip of your tongue" and just couldn't recall it, no matter how hard you tried. After several hours, when you thought you'd forgotten all about it, it suddenly "popped" into your mind; you suddenly remembered it. It *didn't* just "pop" into your mind. When you thought you'd forgotten about it, your subconscious continued to work until it solved the problem for you, reintroducing it into your conscious.

The power and potential of the problem-solving mechanism in the subconscious is awesome. For example, in order to compute where a ball will fall, a center-fielder must take into account the speed of the ball, its curvature of fall, its direction, wind velocity and direction, initial velocity, and the rate of progressive decrease in velocity. He must make these computations so that he will be able to take off at the crack of the bat.

In addition, he must compute just how fast he needs to run and in what direction in order to meet the ball when it lands. The center-fielder doesn't even think about this. His built-in problem-solving mechanism computes it for him from data which he feeds it through his eyes and ears. The computer in his brain takes this information, compares it with stored information (memories of previous successes and failures in catching fly balls), and makes all the necessary computations in a flash before ordering his leg muscles to run.

Your subconscious will go to work, providing answers for problems, if you'll just relax, open up, and let it. It has answers to questions you don't even know you have.

3. The third function of the subconscious is to *control* all automatic bodily functions, such as breathing, digestion, circulation, etc. It maintains and preserves the well-being and life of our bodies. We don't have to think about breathing, let alone all the other automatic functions, because the subconscious takes care of them for us.

4. Finally, the subconscious mind *releases energy* to achieve our goals. One of the most exciting things that I've read in a long time is a report which says that the minute you or I get a written goal for ourselves, a flow of energy is released into the body that allows us to start doing the things necessary to reach that goal.

However, as stated earlier, this mechanism will also work against you. Present it with negative goals and it operates just as impersonally and just as faithfully as a failure mechanism.

Zig Ziglar, motivational speaker, personal friend, and author of *See You at the Top*, decided to practice what he preaches. A few years ago, he decided he needed to lose thirty-four pounds. That was his first step—setting the goal of thirty-four pounds. The next thing he did was stop eating cottage cheese. He did this because he thought that only overweight people ate cottage cheese. All he had to do was eat it, and he would be telling his subconscious he was fat; the very thing he did not want it to hear.

Zig then decided to get a mental picture of what he wanted to look like after he lost weight; so, he got out an old photo of himself from his slimmer days and put it on his refrigerator door. Each day he looked at that picture and said, "That's what I'm going to look like." He programmed his mind until he actually began to see himself that way. In other words, he began to see what it would feel like to be thin again. He eventually started acting as though he were thin.

Over a period of time Zig lost his thirty-four pounds. He

didn't push a button in the mind called the "Willpower Button." He simply took control of his mind by programming it positively. Perhaps that's what willpower is, after all. He made a decision, set a goal, and created a mental picture of what he wanted; his mind took over and did the rest. It released the energy necessary for him to achieve his goal.

Psychologists tell us that a person talks to himself at a rate of thirteen hundred words per minute; and as far as your subconscious is concerned, what you say to yourself is true. I may lie to my wife, my daughter, my sons, my son-in-law, my daughter-in-law, or my friends, but I can't lie to myself. If I say it's true, it's true. So every time you tell yourself something, you've practically created a memory pattern—your mind has already heard it three times: when you thought it, when you said it, and when you heard it.

The subconscious can't discern between real and imagined, or fantasized, experiences. So be very careful about your daydreams and thoughts. An imagined experience is vividly recorded on the subconscious forever. That's why it's so important to think positively, to talk to yourself in positive ways, and to get positive mental pictures of what you want to be, of what you want to do, of what you want to look like, and of what you want to accomplish. It's only then that your subconscious will really go to work for you in positive, not negative, ways.

Understanding how the mind works is the first step toward understanding your self-image and why you behave and react in certain ways. The mind can do great things for you. But if you program it with negative, self-destructive images and thoughts, it can also work against you. It is the repository for those things you place in it which say, "This is who I am." The good news is that if you do have low self-esteem, it can be changed. *Anyone can be a winner!*

5

"THE ME I SEE IS THE ME I'LL BE"

THE YEAR WAS 1953. Little eight-year-old Susan stood before her third-grade class in total embarrassment. She'd come to school that morning in a state of excitement and pride. She had something to show her classmates and teacher that would prove she was the same as they were, that she had nice things just as they did.

Susan's father was a tenant farmer and could scarcely afford the twenty-five cents per day for school lunches for each of his three school-age daughters. The school allowed the girls to charge their lunches each day until their father could pay the bill at the end of each month. They wore clothing handed down from older sisters that had been purchased in second-hand clothing stores. They sat with their friends at recess and listened to them talking about their favorite TV programs. Susan and her two sisters had never even seen a TV before. They spent all their spare time doing chores on

69

the farm; and when they did have some leisure time, all they had for entertainment was each other and a small brown radio full of static.

It was no wonder that this little eight-year-old glowed with pride when a kind neighbor gave her a practically new winter coat her daughter had outgrown. The beautiful emerald green coat sported an imitation fur collar which tickled Susan's neck. And to this little girl who knew what it was like to be poor, it was a symbol that now she was just as important as her friends.

It was with this excitement that she rushed into her classroom the next morning, wearing her new coat and glowing with pride. She immediately showed her teacher her new prize. The teacher didn't waste any time telling little Susan what she thought.

"Susan, do you mean to tell me that your parents can't afford to pay for your lunch each day, but they can afford to buy you a new coat?"

All of Susan's protestations and explanations fell on deaf ears. Her teacher simply refused to believe that a coat looking as new as this one could have been given to a poor little farm girl. She continued her insults, finally sending Susan to her seat in tears.

Susan's new coat, the source of her excitement and pride—instead of buying her some respect from her teacher and peers—had turned out to be yet another cause for embarrassment. As she sat in her seat choking back the tears, Susan wondered if it would ever be possible for her to feel like everyone else, to be like everyone else, and to have the things that everyone else had. Feeling alone and outcast, she wondered if there would ever be a time when she wouldn't be ridiculed and embarrassed over things that weren't even her fault.

This experience was only one of many which contributed to the formation of little Susan's self-image. Her teacher could have turned this experience into something very positive, helping Susan feel important and accepted. But she, like many teachers, parents, and friends, chose the opposite course of action. And however innocent this teacher's actions and words may have been, they had a lifelong impact on how

Susan saw herself as a person, and how she viewed her worth to the world around her.

For people like Susan, as well as for you and me, there is hope. But before we can change our own self-images, it is important that we understand the sources of those images; not only that we may better understand ourselves, but also that we may comprehend the effect our actions and words may have on others.

PARENTS, TEACHERS, PEERS

The first way people get pictures of themselves is through their parents, teachers, and peers. As I said in chapter 4, through an empathetic process, a baby begins to feel loved or unloved even before it's born. After a baby is born, everything that happens to it and everything that's said to it will affect how it sees itself as a person later in life. We actually begin to determine who and what we are based upon what our parents, teachers, and peers tell us by their words and show us by their actions.

We *begin* to get a picture of ourselves through experiences with our parents, teachers, and peers because they are the first to influence us in the earliest stages of life. You and I are programmed based upon what they tell or don't tell us, on how they make us feel, and on what they show or don't show us by their actions. Parents, teachers, and peers can adversely affect children in five ways.

1. The first way a person's self-image is influenced by parents, teachers, and peers is through *negative, destructive criticism*. The negative criticism we've received throughout our lifetimes has had an impact on each of our self-images. On the other hand, we have affected the self-esteem of our children, spouses, and friends through negative criticism of their actions, grades, behavior, appearance, performance and opinions.

Children look up to their parents as though they were God. Anything they say is taken as gospel truth. If a child's parents tell him or her something, the child thinks it must be true. Children take all remarks, looks, actions, implications, and insinuations, storing them deep in the subconscious mind in a file marked "WHO I AM."

For example, little Larry brought home an F on a report card. These are the remarks he received from his parents: "What, another F? Larry, you never make good grades in math. Can't you ever make even one good grade? You aren't very good in math, are you? You aren't even going to pass math. I guess you'll never be able to make a decent math grade."

Larry's parents love him. They want him to make good grades and succeed in life. They were trying to tell him that they were unhappy with his grades and that he had to do better in order to pass. But they weren't really *saying* that. Between the lines, they were telling their son he was dumb. That's all he heard; that's what registered on his subconscious. He heard that he was dumb, that he couldn't pass math, and that he could never make a decent grade. And because his parents said it, it had to be true.

Dr. George Hall says that a person must hear something six times before it registers on the mind, forms an emgram, and becomes a part of the memory pattern. After six bad report cards, or even six bad parental remarks, Larry began to believe that he could never do any better. The next time he made an F in math, he thought, "Daddy always said I was dumb. I guess he's right."

It's not the criticism that's at fault here. It's the fact that it's *negative* criticism. To help change a person's behavior, positive, or constructive, criticism should be used. Positive criticism should include support, encouragement, acceptance, and belief in the other person's capabilities and talents.

For example, Larry's parents could have chosen to say, "Larry, since you made an F in math, we find it necessary to ground you. You know that we have a rule in this family that says each of us must live up to his potential. The reason we're grounding you is not because we think you're dumb. It's because we know you're not doing what you're capable of doing. You know it and we know it. You're too smart to be making Fs in math. We expect you to make much better grades than this. We want you to live up to your potential. Perhaps the extra study time you'll have by being grounded will provide the opportunity you need to bring up this grade. We love you very much, and we know that you're capable of doing much better."

Experts have said that we could totally restructure the grade levels of achievement of our students within one generation if teachers and parents would just learn to use positive reinforcement and constructive criticism. Dr. William Glasser helped raise the grade point average of an entire class by one whole point by simply walking into class every morning and saying, "Everyone in this class can make an A today. Isn't that great? Now, let's see what we can do to earn it."

Those students began to get a picture of what they could do. After hearing it every day, they started to believe it was actually possible. They began to anticipate success. Their subconscious minds worked in their favor by helping them change their behavior and achieve that success.

Destructive criticism robs a person of his or her sense of worth because the *person* has been criticized, not the behavior or performance. On the other hand, constructive criticism enables a person to discover his or her personhood through encouragement, positive reinforcement, and acceptance. There is always a positive way to criticize.

2. The second way parents, teachers, and peers influence a person's self-image is through *unfair comparisons*. This happens when a person insists on comparing a spouse, a child, an employee, a student with someone else. Here are some examples.

Wife: "Why can't you be as successful as Joe across the street? He buys his wife whatever she needs. Why can't you do that?"

Parent: "Bobby is going to be the tall one in the family. I don't understand why you aren't as tall as Bobby. I guess you're just going to be the runt in the family."

Teacher: "Why can't you make good grades like your brother did? I never had the problem with him that I have with you. He was such a pleasure to teach. You should be as smart as your brother. After all, you're from the same family."

Why do people take the worst characteristics of one person and compare them with the best characteristics of another? The first person is never going to look good when this happens, not to mention how it will make him feel. It's unfair. When people are always made to feel that they're only second best, it's no wonder that they go through life feeling inadequate and out of place, never being able to live up to their potential.

I have a friend who went through high school as an A and B student. She belonged to all the right clubs, served on the student council, and edited the school yearbook her senior year. When her younger sister followed her and turned out to be a C student who wasn't interested in the same things, the teachers couldn't understand why. Through four agonizing years of high school, this younger sister constantly heard, "Why can't you be more like your sister?" from her teachers.

Years later, the younger sister went to work for the company where her older sister had worked for two years. Her boss was a witty and easygoing person who liked to joke around. Meaning no harm, he constantly called her "Kathy's sister" instead of calling her by her own name.

Finally, one day she'd had enough and blew up at him. "I have a name!" she shouted. "I am me and no one else. If you can't use my name, don't even talk to me!"

Her boss, unaware of what he'd been doing, offered his apology. From then on, he used her given name when talking with her. But others haven't been so fortunate.

Each person should be measured by his or her own abilities and talents, not by someone else's. You're the only person you need to compete with in order to be successful. You should always be trying to exceed the things you've done before.

Galatians 6:4 (TLB) says, "Let everyone be sure that he is doing his very best, for then he will have the personal satisfaction of work well done, and won't need to compare himself with someone else."

The most successful people are those who decide what and who they want to be. They go after it, without comparing themselves to other people, using their own talents and abilities to achieve their goals. Such success has no dollar value on it. It's simply a result of realizing you're your own person and that you don't need to compete against others in order to be successful.

3. Parents, teachers, and peers also adversely influence a person's self-image through *rejection*. This is the toughest one to handle. In chapter 4, I said that before a person is thirty years old, he or she will have three trillion memories recorded in the subconscious mind. Remember the girl who wouldn't date you in high school? That's recorded in your mind forever. Remember the football player you liked so much, but who never asked you out? That's etched in your memory as well. Remember the club, sorority, or fraternity that wouldn't let you in? That's in there, too.

Remember the times when you came in at midnight and had an 11:00 curfew? Mom would be sitting on the sofa, waiting for you. She'd give you that "look." My mother really had the knack. She'd look at me and her chin would quiver. But she'd never say anything. I'd go to my room and pray that I could stay one more night without her kicking me out. The silent treatment is hard for anyone to take. The experience of rejection is carved in your memory forever.

A pastor friend once told me the story of a sixteen-year-old girl who came into his office one morning, crying hysterically. It took him forty minutes just to calm her down so that she could tell him what was wrong.

As a fourteen-year-old, she was involved with a young man of whom her father didn't approve. He overreacted to the situation—as fathers so often do—and the result was an explosive, violent argument between the father and his daughter. He told her that she was a tramp, an embarrassment to the family; that she'd ruined her life and his life as well, and that now he would have to leave the church because of her. Later in the argument, he told her that she would have to leave instead. Then he sent her to her room until he could decide on a home or a school to send her to. At the tender age of fourteen, and in desperate need of her father's help, love, and understanding, this young girl was devastated. Her father's rejection drove her to climb out her bedroom window and run away.

Two years later she learned that her mother was dying of cancer. She wanted to go home and see her. Remembering her father's last words, and feeling desperate, she sought out the pastor for advice. He telephoned her father and told him that his daughter was in his office wanting to come home to see her mother. The father was elated. He told the pastor to tell his daughter that he could come for her immediately.

When the pastor relayed her father's message, this frightened, grief-stricken sixteen-year-old runaway said, "No way! He'll put me in a reform school or a convent. I can't possibly go home."

The scotoma, or the blind spot, which we discussed in chapter 4, was working on this young girl. She believed what she "saw," what *appeared* to her as the truth. The fact that her father didn't want her was no longer true, but it remained true to her. She'd heard her father tell her she was a tramp enough times that it had made a permanent imprint on her mind. She believed that he still felt that way; nothing he said could convince her otherwise.

We form opinions of ourselves based partly upon the times when we've experienced rejection. Satan delights in convincing people that they're unworthy, that they're less than they're meant to be. Don't let him fool you. God has promised in John 6:37 that he'll never reject anyone: "But some will come to me—those the Father has given me—and I will never, never reject them" (TLB).

4. Parents, teachers, and peers influence a person's self-image through *self-deprecation*. This happens when one person puts another person down by making him feel as if he owes his total existence to that person.

Parent: "Lee, do you have any idea how I've sacrificed for you? Don't you realize what I've given up so that you can have the things you have and do the things you do? How can you act like this after all I've done for you? Why, if it weren't for me, you wouldn't even be here!"

A child, after hearing this from a parent five or six times, finally decides that he or she is unworthy. Children who are constantly bombarded with self-deprecation feel that they're lucky just to be in the family. They also begin to carry a lot of guilt, feeling that if it weren't for them, their parents would have more and be able to do more than they have and do now. They've been shamed into thinking that they're less than nothing, not worthy of anyone's love.

Parents need to realize that self-sacrifice is a responsibility of parenthood; they should not shift it to the shoulders of innocent children. Children don't ask to be born into a specific family. Making them feel responsible and guilty for their own birth results in a communication breakdown between parent and child because trust and feelings of worthiness and acceptance have been destroyed. Once again, the child's self-image has been fed with negative programming— he has been told that he is a burden, that it's his fault he's a burden, and that he's unworthy of his parents' affection, time, attention, and love.

5. The fifth and final way a person's self-image is adversely influenced by parents, teachers, and peers is through an *unrealistic view of failure*. I think one of the saddest things that parents and teachers have done to children during the present generation is rob them of their right to fail. In expecting perfection, we've taken from our children the necessary experiences of being able to fail, coming back and trying again (perhaps several times), and then finally succeeding. There can be great joy in realizing such success. Somehow, in the past twenty-five years, people have decided that a person who fails is a failure. What a ridiculous lie! The following examples illustrate how a realistic view of failure can result in success.

Walt Disney experienced both bankruptcy and a tragic nervous breakdown. In fact, he was bankrupt when he took his "Steamboat Willie" cartoon idea to Hollywood in 1928. Parents all over the world are grateful that Walt Disney didn't view himself as a failure and give up. Disney stated publicly that bankruptcy was his greatest lesson in life. He must have learned a lot, because children's entertainment has never been the same since. The wonderful cartoon characters, books, amusement parks, television specials, and films all reflect his creative genius.

I know of a young man who was born into a family of twenty-four brothers and sisters, all of whom lived in unbelievable poverty. His father was an alcoholic, and his mother died when he was only five years old. Because he lived a life of crime, he spent most of his youth in reform schools and jails. Hungry for attention and affection, he spent most of his leisure time using his marvelous sense of humor to make people laugh.

When he became a young man, he decided that he wanted to be someone who could touch the lives of others. As his life began to change, his dreams grew larger *and* looked more realistic to him. He began to commit himself to a new, exciting, and rewarding goal. Today, Flip Wilson is a professional comedian. He is in demand across the country—in night clubs, on college campuses, and has recorded dozens of comedy albums.

On the night of December 9, 1914, Edison Industries of West Orange, New Jersey, burned to the ground. Thomas Edison lost $2 million that evening as much of his life's work went up in flames. His "invention factory" had been insured for only $238,000 because it was constructed of concrete, a material then thought to be fireproof.

Twenty-four-year-old Charles Edison was frantic as he searched for his father. Fearing the worst, Charles finally found him standing near the fire, his white hair blowing in the cold December wind and his face ruddy from the glow of the roaring flames.

"My heart ached for him," Charles said. "He was sixty-seven years old—no longer a young man—and everything he'd worked for was going up in smoke."

When the elder Edison spotted his son coming toward him, he shouted, "Charles, where's your mother?"

Charles responded that he didn't know. At that point, Thomas exclaimed, "Find her and bring her here. She'll never see anything like this again as long as she lives!"

The next morning, as Thomas Edison walked through the charred embers of all his hopes and dreams, he told his family, "There is a great value in disaster. It burns up all our mistakes! Thank God we can start anew."

Three months after that devastating fire, Edison Industries presented the world with its first phonograph.

Thomas Edison had perseverance, confidence, a positive attitude, and he refused to accept failure as determinative. He faced adversity head-on. He knew that sixty-seven years and the loss of a business meant nothing because he always had the opportunity to "start anew."

Earlier in his career, Thomas Edison had made over nine hundred attempts before he was able to perfect the electric light bulb.

After failing so many times, his assistant asked, "Do you know that we've failed over nine hundred times?"

"No, no, no," Edison replied emphatically. "We've just found over nine hundred ways that won't work!"

The only time a person can't afford to fail is the very last time she tries. The fact that a person fails doesn't mean that she is a failure. It only means that the person didn't reach her goal at a particular time. Failure can build character, perseverance, ambition, drive, patience, and faith. And turning failure into success builds satisfaction, self-confidence, and fulfillment.

By expecting perfection in our children, we're programming their self-images in a way which tells them they can never be worthwhile. This is so because they will never be able to live up to our expectations of perfection. Who could?

Failure is never final! Children should be made to feel that no matter how hard they try, no matter how many things go wrong, and no matter how many times they fail, someone still loves them, believes in them, and will be there to encourage them to try again. Failure is never final.

OTHERS' EXPECTATIONS

The second way in which people get a view of themselves is through others' expectations and opinions of them. So many times we feel we aren't all we're supposed to be; we sense our loved ones, peers, and associates expect things from us that we aren't prepared to give or aren't capable of giving.

Many people spend their entire lives trying to live up to others' expectations, trying to become the image of what is acceptable. As a result, they never become aware of who they really are. In this case, we aren't who we think we are—we are who we think other people think we are.

In his book, *Having Fun Being Yourself,* Dr. James Keelan suggests a view of ourselves as being a type of balanced, pyramid-shaped scale.[1] In the far left corner is the need to belong, sometimes resulting in the adoption of a "role" in order to fit in. Fad groups of past decades can well illustrate that need: the "flappers" of the twenties, the "beatniks" of the fifties, the "hippies" of the sixties, etc. In trying to be one of the group, people became lost in a crowd, sometimes at the expense of their own individuality.

In the far right corner of the scale is the liberal thinker—the person who has a need to be different and unique. This "do your own thing" philosophy was popular in the seventies. When a person ends up in either corner, the result is an unbalanced, unfulfilled person with a troubled self-image.

In between the two extremes is the center position which maintains a balance for the whole. Here is the real self, the real you, the unique and special person you really are. Here is the person who has "attained belonging because people like him for himself and not for a role."[2] And yet, he still experiences the joy of being different and special. This person is happy with himself.

Society sets standards about how we should look. TV commercials put perfect bodies in front of us, telling us to drink diet sodas. Commercials show models wearing expensive designer jeans, insinuating that we can't look good unless we wear them as well. They tell us what shampoo, toothpaste, and deodorant to use, what food to eat, what clothes and cologne to wear, etc. If we don't follow their suggestions, we won't look good, have friends, and be popular.

Advertisements hook you into buying a product by making you think you can look just like the models you see; models who have daily access to hairdressers, makeup artists, and fashion designers. Then, when you fail to achieve someone else's standard of appearance, you feel inferior, less than acceptable to the world. The people who look like models have spent a lot of time and money to look that way. We tend to forget that they make up a very small percentage of the population. If you have any doubts, take some time to watch the crowds in a busy shopping mall on a Saturday afternoon. See how many people you can find who look as though they just stepped out of an ad.

There's nothing wrong with wanting to belong, to be and look like your friends. Human beings are basically social creatures and seek out others with the same likes and interests. However, when we tend to follow the values of others in order to gain acceptance, we are acting out of fear that we won't be accepted for ourselves and for our own values and priorities in life. Therein lies the danger.

Your ultimate importance to others and to God isn't based on how much you conform or "fit in," nor on your physical appearance. It's based on your individuality and on what's inside your heart. In our need to be accepted and liked, we sometimes forget the importance of this and abandon our individuality to try to live up (or down) to what others expect of us. Maltz says,

> Over-conforming, too much a part of modern life, is something entirely different (than the basic measure of conformity necessary in a civilized life). It is a sacrifice of individual identity when this surrender accomplishes no worthwhile purpose.[3]

When God measures the greatness of an individual, he puts the tape measure around the heart, not the head or the body. He doesn't measure how much we are like others. In 1 Samuel 16:7, God sent Samuel to choose Saul's successor to the throne. God told him,

> Don't judge by a man's face or height, for this is not the one. I don't make decisions the way you do! Men judge by outward appearance, but I look at a man's thoughts and intentions" (TLB).

81

Samuel passed over Jesse's seven handsome eldest sons, in favor of the youngest—the shepherd boy David, the man after God's own heart.

The things that make you unique and different, that set you apart and distinguish you from others, are your characteristics, your emotions, your abilities, your values, your talents, your attitudes, your beliefs, your desires, and your goals in life. These are the things that make you special. These are the reasons why people like or dislike you. These are the things that make you *you*.

WE LIVE IN A NEGATIVE SOCIETY

The third way people get pictures of who they are is through the negative society in which they live. People can take one of three paths in life: one that leads to success, one that leads to failure, and one that leads to mediocrity. The path to mediocrity is not only the most dangerous, it's also the easiest. Why? Because it doesn't cost anything. Therefore, many people have committed themselves to mediocrity and to being unsuccessful. In addition, they don't want others to be successful either. You see, it's much easier for me to go home and explain to my wife that I'm a failure because everyone else is than for me to explain to her why my neighbor is successful and I'm not. That's the tough one.

There are people who are always willing to tell you your problems, your faults, your sins. Not only that, they are also willing to help you find your level of mediocrity. Because they aren't successful, they can't believe that you can be either. They'll discourage you and try to talk you out of new adventures and challenges, all because they don't want you to succeed. Your success can make them look more like failures, and they don't want that.

One of the reasons we live in a negative society is because of the news element. Paul Harvey once told me that 92.7 percent of the news each day is negative. You may have to think awhile before you can remember the last time you read good news on the front page of the newspaper.

Many people begin their day by reading the paper before

or during breakfast. Even before their first cup of coffee, people have read about riots, rapes, murders, bombings, etc. They haven't even had breakfast and they are already reading about terrible things. Perhaps some of them leave their homes feeling depressed, discouraged, and frightened.

I turn on the radio in the morning and hear that we have a 20 percent chance of rain. Why don't we have an 80 percent chance for sunshine? The odds are better for sun. It doesn't make sense. When I drive my car, I have to stop for a stop light. Why don't they call it a "go" light? Isn't its purpose to make traffic flow, not jam? If you receive a telegram, the first thing you may think is, "Who died?" Why? Because we've been conditioned to think negatively.

But, the secret is we don't *have* to live that way. One person may not be able to change the environment or society, but he can change himself and his attitudes toward society and life in general.

A few years ago I was in North Carolina for a speaking engagement. As I was driving through the countryside, enjoying the beautiful, rolling hills lined with pine trees, I came upon the town where I was scheduled to speak. Posted at its city limits was a large sign which read, "WE HEAR THERE'S A RECESSION COMING AND WE'VE DECIDED NOT TO PARTICIPATE!" I liked that!

As I walked into the Chamber of Commerce banquet that evening, I could feel the electricity in the air. It was contagious. It seemed as though these people weren't concerned with the negative news that they'd heard. They were having a good time, making successful things happen for themselves and for their community. They refused to let negative thinking and the events of the world around them program them.

SELF-TALK

The fourth and final way people get pictures of who they are is through self-talk.

Remember that the mind has to hear something only six times before it becomes fixed in the memory forever. Perhaps you've gone on a diet fifteen times and lost the same ten pounds fifteen times. If so, you've probably said at least six times fifteen times that you just can't seem to lose weight. No wonder! Your mind has heard it so much that it believes it, and your subconscious makes you behave in such a way as to make it true. If you "can't" do something, and then you turn around and do it, your mind is in immediate conflict and confusion because you've lied to it. Your subconscious will not be able to understand that you *can* lose weight. If you say it, it's true to your subconscious whether it's true in reality or not.

Do you get up in the morning, look in the mirror, and say, "Oh, I look terrible"? It's no wonder. You just said you did, so your mind believed it!

When a friend compliments you on a dress you're wearing, do you say, "Oh, this old thing?"

When you make a mistake, do you say, "Oh, I'm so dumb. I can't do anything right"? If you do, beware, because you'll eventually begin to believe that you can't do anything right. Your mind will start promoting behavior to prove you're right about yourself.

Self-criticism is the most destructive, dangerous method of negative programming. If people can talk to themselves at a rate of thirteen hundred words per minute, it's no wonder this method sticks! By using it, you're programming yourself to believe that you're less than you are. You're only hurting yourself.

Adults as well as children need encouragement, and sometimes we must give it to ourselves. Self-talk should always be positive and encouraging: "I need to practice more or try harder next time. I can do better than that." (Chapter 8 will deal with positive self-talk in more detail.)

Of self-talk, Maltz writes,

> The aim of self-image psychology is not to create a fictitious self which is omnipotent. Such an image is as untrue as the inferior image of oneself. Our aim is to find the best we have in us, realistically, and to bring it out into the open. Why should you continue to short-change yourself?[4]

Most of us never discover that real person deep within us, because we're hampered by what our parents, teachers, and peers have told us over the years. The negative programming that is all around us, our own negative self-talk, and the unrealistic expectations of others all contribute to the difficulties we have about letting anything positive enter our minds. It's life-damaging to dwell on past failures and disappointments.

You can turn your whole life around by using positive reinforcement—by reliving in your mind your successes, your accomplishments, your awards, your victories, and your triumphs. How sad that so many people don't know this and go through life believing untruths and other people's opinions of them. Many never discover their own potential and abilities. And many never become what they've dreamed of becoming or what they were created to be. *Anyone can be a winner!*

6

FEAR IS A DARKROOM WHERE NEGATIVES ARE DEVELOPED

MY DRIVER RAN yellow and red lights, darting in and out of traffic in a desperate attempt to get me to the airport in time for my flight. I'd just finished another speaking engagement, and my host had been kind enough to provide me with a car and driver so I wouldn't miss my plane.

The driver pulled to a screeching halt in a no parking zone directly in front of the terminal's main doors. I knew it was a no parking zone, but I didn't say anything to him because I was in a great hurry and the car was only going to be there for a few seconds—just long enough for me to hop out, retrieve my luggage, and head for the nearest door. My driver opened the trunk of the car and handed my luggage to me. As I turned to head for the door, I nearly collided with a uniformed policeman.

Standing there with his hands on his hips, the officer started shouting, obviously not interested in any explanations. He vented his anger primarily on the young driver, a man barely out of his teens. The things the policeman said to him were unbelievable. The driver stood rooted to the pavement, staring at the officer in disbelief.

Finally, when the policeman paused for a breath, my driver said, "Sir, has someone ruined your day?"

"What?" the policeman replied with surprise.

"Sir has someone done something to make you feel bad about yourself? May I help you?"

The policeman, totally shocked by this unexpected response to his violent outburst, muttered, "Take your time." Then he turned and slowly walked away.

"My gosh, Mr. Timberlake, it works!" my driver exclaimed excitedly.

That young man had just heard me speak and had obviously listened very closely. The policeman wasn't mad at the driver as a person. He didn't even know him. But, something had gone wrong for him that day. His wife had fought with him, the neighbor's dog had bitten him, his commanding officer had chewed him out, or something else had happened to him to make him angry, to make him want to strike back at the next person who crossed his path. That next person just happened to be my young driver.

The officer, mad at the world for some unknown reason, saw his chance to vent his anger, to relieve himself of his frustrations. He could have ruined that young man's whole day except for one thing—the driver recognized that the policeman had a problem and chose not to let it become his problem as well. Unfortunately, most of us don't do that.

In chapter 3, I described the process that evolves from the central self-image in the subconscious, to the ultimate behavior resulting from it. In other words, your behavior is a direct reflection of your self-image. The young driver recognized that the policeman's negative behavior suggested that he didn't like himself. You can gradually learn to determine the way a person feels about herself simply by observing her behavior patterns.

The rest of this chapter will discuss seven essential ways a person with low self-esteem acts. The most important thing to remember, however, is that when people behave or react negatively toward you, it usually isn't because they don't like you; rather, it's because they don't like themselves. If you can realize this, then you've taken a step toward understanding two basic truths. First, persons who consistently attack others are doing so because of their own insecurities and negative feelings about themselves. Second, their frustrations and negative feelings aren't your problems.

People with low self-esteem are simply acting out of fear; a fear that they're worthless and unlovable. As stated before, we know that fear is a darkroom where negatives are developed. Such feelings of unworthiness soon develop into negative behavior projected toward others. The moment someone else hurts them, their first impulse is to strike out at others, because hurting people hurt other people.

FEELINGS OF BEING A "NOBODY"

First of all, people with low self-esteem are preoccupied with feelings of being a nobody. They are consumed with the idea that they aren't important to themselves or to anyone else. They continually engage in negative self-talk and spend a lot of time telling other people how worthless they are.

Once, after conducting a seminar for some engineers at an IBM location in Florida, I met a young woman who asked to speak to me after the session.

"I'm engaged to marry a man who works here," she began. "He's a brilliant engineer with a promising career. The problem is he doesn't believe he's capable of all that he really is capable of. I couldn't even get him to come and hear you today. He said it wasn't any use because there's no way he's going to make it anyway. He's committed to the idea that he's a loser and that he'll never be successful. He thinks no one likes him. We probably won't get married because he's convinced he'll never be able to support a family, and that I can never possibly care for him as much as he cares for me."

That's a perfect picture of a person with low self-esteem. He begins the day knowing things will go wrong and doesn't

even try to make them go right. He doesn't want to be bothered with anyone telling him he's wrong, or with anyone
trying to encourage him in any way.

This preoccupation with feelings of worthlessness results
in two specific behavior patterns:

1. There is an *expectation of rejection, humiliation, and
failure.* People with low self-esteem expect others to break
in line ahead of them, or others to be served before them in
a restaurant. And if it does happen, they say, "Oh, I knew
it!"

They'll spot you sitting at a table in the cafeteria at work
and walk up and ask, "May I sit here?"

"I'm saving this seat for my wife. She's joining me for lunch
today," you reply.

"Well, I knew you didn't want me to sit with you. I knew
you'd treat me that way. Why don't you like me?" they'll ask
as they walk away in a huff, never accepting the fact that
what you've told them is the truth.

2. People with feelings of worthlessness are *cowed by
other people.* They are the "doormats" of society. They allow
themselves to be run over and abused by others because they
honestly feel they don't deserve better treatment. They will
never stand up for what they believe, but instead agree with
everything and anything they're told. They will always settle
for second best.

CRITICISM AND FAULT-FINDING

The second way some people reflect a poor self-image is
through criticism and fault-finding. They constantly, consistently, and continually criticize. The majority of the population doesn't care about your problems, and the rest are glad
you've got them. They can isolate and describe your problem
in great detail, but will never offer any suggestions toward
a solution. And nothing is ever done quickly enough or well
enough to satisfy them.

These people are the first to yell at the umpire in a baseball
game, to chew out a waitress and make a scene in a restau-

rant, or to talk out loud and complain throughout a movie. They're always finding fault, because putting people down is the only way they can draw attention to themselves and make themselves feel good.

You may read a good motivational book or hear a good speech and go away feeling much better about yourself, your life, your family, and your God. But when you share this with a friend or neighbor who has low self-esteem, you hear, "Are you kidding? That isn't the real world. How do you think you can be anyone special? Those people don't know you like I do."

People like this don't want you to make it. They think *they* can't make it. And so the only way they can feel better about themselves is to constantly criticize and find fault with others. It's their way of trying to prove to themselves and to the world that they're important, that they count, too.

INTOLERANT OF CRITICISM

Third, the very people who are the first to criticize are the last to accept criticism. They're very intolerant of *any* criticism, positive or negative. If you offer them any criticism, they'll turn it around, redirecting it at you because they think they're always right. You can't tell them anything.

A second symptom of their intolerance for criticism is an explosive temper. They'll blow up at the drop of a hat. They don't have the strength within themselves to discuss things rationally; so they must outshout you to make up for it. And here's why: They can't tell the difference between their person and their performance. As a result, they take everything personally. They're always on the defensive.

People enjoy talking to me after I speak. A lot of them offer compliments and praise. I'm happy when they do. It's nice to know that I've accomplished my objective and helped someone in some way. But, there are others who love to tell me that I misquoted someone, that my grammar isn't what it should be, that I got a statistic wrong, etc.

When I first started speaking for a living, I'd periodically feel like giving up, because so many people would line up to criticize me. Then one day I realized that they weren't attacking me, they were criticizing my performance. It wasn't *me* they didn't like. They were simply offering constructive criticism, trying to help me improve. I needed to improve. (And still do.) There was no reason for me to get upset, depressed, and give up over a little constructive criticism. When people react emotionally, they are saying, "I don't like myself, and you just proved I'm right by being critical of me." They can't discern the difference between their person and their performance.

LOVE TO GOSSIP

People with a poor self-image love to gossip and keep rumors alive. Their favorite words are, "Let me tell you, honey." Gossip is merely one person's way of spreading other people's misery in order to make himself or herself feel good. And these people can tell you exactly what's happening to whom and who's doing what, where, and how.

Gossip is a leveler. This means that if I can't get up to my neighbor's level, I'll pull her down to mine by spreading gossip and rumors about her. A gossip takes great joy in the misery of others. By allowing himself to be consumed in the misery of others, a gossip has found a way to make himself feel good. That's why so many people like to watch TV soap operas. People on these programs can make his problems look small in comparison.

Paul Harvey once told me that a company in Illinois— Good News America—recently went bankrupt after being in business only four years. He told me this happened because people didn't want to hear any good news. That's shameful. People would rather hear about the misery of others than hear about all the good things that are going on around them every day.

We should be wary of such people. Proverbs 20:19 says that unless we want everyone to know what we've said, we shouldn't associate with gossips.

JEALOUS AND INSECURE

Everything frightens insecure people. Everything is a threat. Everything is a problem. If they go to a football game, they'll swear that the offensive team in the huddle on the field is talking about them. If a conversation suddenly comes to a halt when they enter a room, they will insist that they were the subject of it. This is the fifth way a person reflects a low self-image.

Psychologists say that insecurity breeds depression. Everyone gets depressed now and then. It's a part of coping with life. But the person with poor self-esteem *stays* depressed. He expects defeat and rejection. Nothing in life matters to him; he thinks it will turn out wrong anyway, so why even try?

This kind of insecurity promotes jealousy. Jealousy is one person's insecurity manifested toward another. If I don't like myself, I won't be secure in my relationships because I'll think that my family and friends don't like me either.

Statistics state that 63 percent of the problems in the workplace are caused by jealousy. Thus, it stands to reason that no man or woman can get a promotion without snide remarks about how he or she got it. It's one person's way of explaining why she made it and he didn't. Women are accused of being involved with the boss; men are accused of lying and cheating to get to the top; and minorities are accused of being given promotions in order to meet government quotas.

The problem doesn't lie with women, blacks, Mexican-Americans, or any other group. The problem lies with insecure people. Because they aren't secure in their own talents and abilities, they're jealous of the talents and abilities of others.

People need to learn to love themselves just as they are. From this self-love, people can accept and love others more easily. That's why Matthew 22:39 commands us to love our neighbors as we love ourselves. It's necessary for us to love ourselves *first*. And if we don't, then it's our responsibility and obligation to ourselves and our families to do something about it.

Insecurity and jealousy lead people to think that they must always compete with someone else in order to be successful. Such people don't have enough self-confidence to believe they can do it on their own, without comparing themselves to anyone else.

A few years ago I was in New York City and had the privilege of watching the New York Marathon. The newspapers reported that Alberto Salazar won that marathon. Alberto Salazar came in first with a time of two hours, twenty-one minutes. But in my opinion, he didn't win. I believe that Cynthia, another runner, won the marathon with a time of eleven hours, twenty-seven minutes. You see, Cynthia has cerebral palsy. She ran the marathon with no back muscles, gaining her only support from a pair of thin, wobbly crutches. She wasn't competing against Mr. Salazar. Cynthia was competing against herself. She had no reason to be jealous and insecure because her objective was simply to endure. And she did!

If people with poor self-esteem could learn who they are inside, what they want out of life, what their hidden talents are, and that no one else has to lose in order for them to win, then they wouldn't have to be jealous and insecure. They wouldn't have to try to hold others back and put others down in order to feel good. Instead they could rest secure in the knowledge that they are special and worthwhile, independent of what other people are and of what others think of them.

SERIOUS RELATIONSHIP PROBLEMS

A person with a poor self-image has a difficult time maintaining meaningful relationships. This can mean two things:

1. *They have a hard time making and keeping friends.* They have no close friends, only acquaintances. Everyone needs at least one person who, no matter what takes place, will be there for him to confide in and depend upon. For some of us, it's our spouse. For others, it's a friend of the same sex. I heard someone once say that "a friend is someone who knows you and likes you anyway."

I conducted a program once for IT & T. When it was over and everyone had filed out of the auditorium, I was approached by someone who handed me a piece of paper on which he'd written his definition of friendship: "Friendship is the suspension of disbelief." I like that. In other words, a friend is that one person who doesn't care what the world believes—he's still on your side. When we don't have that kind of friend, life can be very tough, leaving us hurting in our solitude.

In 1983 the show business industry recognized the twentieth anniversary of the death of actress Marilyn Monroe. Television offered documentaries and movies about her life. Tributes were made to her in Hollywood. Newspapers carried interviews with people who had known her best.

One morning, Tom Ewell was a guest on ABC's "Good Morning America." He had co-starred with Marilyn in *The Seven Year Itch*. "Good Morning America" host, David Hartman, asked Mr. Ewell to share the one thing that he'd never forget about Marilyn Monroe.

Tom Ewell shared a story about the producers and directors giving a celebration party on the day the filming of *The Seven Year Itch* ended. Everyone who had anything at all to do with the filming had been invited. When the director invited Marilyn, he told her that she could bring a friend if she liked.

"I don't have a friend," she responded. Twenty-eight years old and no friend.

People without close friends go through life as loners, as did Marilyn Monroe. They won't go out because they don't enjoy or feel comfortable in crowds. They won't participate in church or social functions because it would take them out of that comfort zone we talked about. They feel that they're not liked, that other people don't care about their opinions; so why should they expose themselves to an uncomfortable and perhaps embarrassing situation?

People with poor self-esteem don't have friends because they are afraid to open up and be honest with anyone. They don't want others to know their hurts, their agonies, their weaknesses, or their failures. They're afraid that if they open up with people, they won't be liked for who they really are.

They can't believe that other people have the same kinds of weaknesses as they do. In order to be liked, they find it necessary to present a facade to the world, an interpretation of what they think the world wants to see.

2. Thus, we shouldn't be surprised that people who have a hard time with meaningful relationships can also *have serious marital problems*. They often believe that if they don't like themselves, no one else can either. Sadly enough, their subconscious will work to prove them right.

I've read numerous reports which itemize the major causes of divorce. The most startling discovery in these reports isn't that there are basically eight to ten major causes, but that each cause is the *result of poor self-esteem* in one or both partners.

Say you visit a doctor for a serious skin infection and all he does is put ointment on it and send you home. Later on you discover that you have skin cancer. Chances are, you wouldn't be very pleased with that doctor's diagnosis, nor impressed with his competency. Obviously, he failed to seek out the source of the infection. But that's just what the experts have been doing with troubled marriages for years. They've been putting bandages on the results without discovering and remedying the cause: a poor self-image.

If I don't like myself, but my wife likes who she is, she'll be more ambitious, more outgoing, and more self-confident than I. She'll want a better home, better clothes, and better things for our children. But I won't think I can provide them. We'll be destined to have problems in our marriage. She will expect things of me that I won't think possible. I'll see her as demanding and she'll see me as apathetic, with no ambition. Our whole life might end up being one long battle, because my ability to see my own potential is hampered by my poor self-image.

On the other hand, if my wife doesn't like herself, but I like who I am, I'll have the desire to work and travel and be involved in life. She'll just want to stay home, away from people sulking in her jealousy of me. She'll want me home at the same time every evening; she'll want to know where I've been, and whom I've talked with. We'll spend our entire married life in frustration and discord. She'll view me as seeking fulfillment outside the home, away from her. She will understand it to mean that I don't want to be around her. I will see her as disinterested in what I want out of life, not willing to do things or go places with me. I will see her as uncaring. Again, our whole life might end up being one long battle.

It's no wonder the divorce rate is 50 percent and climbing. People with low self-esteem won't try to do better because they think there is no hope. Can you imagine what a marriage is like in which both partners have low self-esteem? Without outside help, that marriage is doomed from the start.

The most difficult thing I have to live with in my travels around the country each week is the fact that my wife trusts me. That's tough. That means she expects me to live by her standards. And because she expects this of me, I want to try very hard to please her. When I get home, she doesn't put me on the spot, going over a list of things I did or didn't do. Why? Because she likes herself and she's secure in our relationship. She thinks I'm lucky to have her, and she's right! She sees herself as someone special, and she has taught me to see myself as someone special, too. Now I think that she's lucky to have me! As a result, both of us enjoy our relationship because we have a mutual respect and trust of each other. We both like who we are and are secure in that. We try hard to make it work. We don't just hang on, waiting and expecting the other to mess up, leave, or stop loving because of some insecurity.

For a marriage to be the beautiful thing God intended it to be, both partners must not only love their respective spouse, they must also love themselves.

APATHETIC TOWARD GOALS

The seventh and final way people with low self-esteem may act is to be terribly fearful of what the future might bring. More importantly, this suggests they are very apathetic toward goals. They will not make plans; and if they were somehow able to, they wouldn't believe the plans would work out anyway. They simply aren't motivated to look beyond today. In fact, most of them are obsessed with the past—it's all they think or talk about. They are secure with the past because they know it. The unknown future presents a frightening threat to them.

Throughout this book, I refer to people who have told me they just can't believe what I say. I've been asked many times if I really believe everything I tell people in my seminars. When I ask these people how they reckon with all the success stories—the people, the names, the dates, the documentation that stands for itself—they usually respond with, "That's the exception to the rule." Then they begin to list endless reasons why goal-setting won't work.

People who won't set goals to work toward and who refuse to believe that goal-setting works try to belittle anyone else who dares to try it. They've given up all hope for themselves. Their self-images are so poor that they don't believe they can succeed with or without goals. And because they don't want to look like the failures they believe themselves to be, they discount any plan for success that others may try. But Proverbs 16:9 states that "We should make plans—counting on God to direct us" (TLB).

Perhaps you've seen yourself, one of your loved ones, or a friend in some of these descriptions. It's not too late to change. If a person's self-image can be positively changed, then his or her behavior will change on its own. But a good self-image is not a destination. Rather, it's a continuous journey. And in order to maintain a good, healthy self-image, you must do what's necessary on a continuing basis. The world isn't going to stop its negative programming, nor are people going to stop trying to pull you down to their levels.

Don't allow anyone else to tell you how to live your life, because you *can* be a winner. If you believe, as the Bible states, that you were created in God's image, how can you think that you're only second best? Is God second best? Does he make mistakes in his creation? You are God's creation, and he wants only the best for you. He promised just that in Jeremiah 29:11: "For I know the plans I have for you, says the Lord. They are plans for good and not for evil, to give you a future and a hope."

You *can* come out of the darkroom of fear. You can come into the light of knowing who you are, of accepting and loving who and what you've found, and of recognizing yourself as someone special. *Anyone can be a winner!*

WHEN I SEE MYSELF
AS A WINNER

A NUMBER OF years ago, a high school in Harlem had a class of "incorrigible" students—young men who "couldn't learn," whose only discipline was meted out by the policemen who were hired to patrol the halls and protect the teachers and other students from periodic outbursts of violence. The school couldn't get teachers to stay in this classroom for more than two to three days before they would resign out of fear for their lives. It seemed an impossible situation for even the most physically fit, intelligent, and brave.

After losing several teachers in a row, the principal requested yet another from the school board. This time they sent a little old lady nearing retirement age. The principal was astounded. How could they send someone like this to handle a class of misfits? Informing her of the type of students she would be teaching, he gave her the opportunity to leave before she even began.

"Absolutely not," she answered. "I don't see as I'll have any problems with these young men."

The principal, unable to share her optimism or to dissuade her, presented her with the class roster and offered to station a policeman in the room as her bodyguard. Again she refused. Reluctant to turn her loose in a room with potential criminals, he finally gave in, vowing to check in on her periodically to see that she was all right.

The principal was amazed to find that she was still at her job by the end of the first week. There had been no major problems in her classroom and no complaints from other teachers or students.

The weeks went by. Each day the principal walked past her classroom where he saw these young men busy at their desks or taking part in some classroom activity. He just couldn't understand how this little old lady could have such a hold on an incorrigible bunch of thugs. It just didn't make sense.

When the first grade reports were issued, it was evident that something had occurred that had never happened in that school before. The group of "incorrigible" students had actually passed! The principal had to find out why.

"Oh, it's simple," the teacher said when asked how she had accomplished this miracle. "I just let them know that boys as smart as they are should do much better than they've been doing. And I also let them know that I wasn't threatened by them because I cared about them."

"What do you mean, 'boys as smart as they are'?" asked the principal.

"You know," she responded. "These boys have exceptionally high IQs. When I saw that, I knew I could help them. They just needed a challenge."

"Where did you get the idea that they had high IQs?" he asked.

"Why, on that class roster you gave me the first day," she answered. "Their IQ numbers were listed beside their names."

Looking somewhat amazed and embarrassed, the principal responded, "Those weren't their IQ numbers. Those were their locker numbers!"

This teacher didn't do anything unusual or extraordinary with her class of problem students. She just began each day by telling them how smart they were and that she cared about them. She told them often enough that they started to believe it. Their self-images were changed in a positive way. And once their self-esteem was raised, their behavior changed accordingly—not because they had high IQs, but because they changed the way they *saw themselves*. They came to realize that they had worth. If you can help change the way a person sees herself, or the way you see yourself, you can help change behavior.

In chapter 6 we learned how a person with low self-esteem behaves. In this chapter we'll take a look at specific characteristics and behavior patterns of people with good, healthy self-images.

LIKE THEMSELVES

People with good self-images believe they are winners. They like who they are and there's no doubt in their minds that they will be successful someday. They feel good about themselves and *believe* in what they're doing.

Many people think that a person with a good self-image will walk into a room feeling he has to be the center of attention. They may think a person with a good self-image is "in love with himself." Not so! That kind of a person has a terrible inferiority complex, or a poor self-image. He's starving for attention and wants to be noticed, many times acting the class clown or the "star" at a party.

A person with a good self-image is comfortable in any situation—with a crowd of people, as the center of attention, or sitting alone in a corner. Such a person doesn't feel threatened by others because he likes who he is and is comfortable with himself. People with high self-esteem may not be where they want to be, but they're on their way.

The Apostle Paul said that he had learned to be content in whatever situation he was in. And yet, he was always striving toward a goal in order to be all that God had intended for him to be. He knew that God might allow him to remain in unpleasant situations until such time as he was ready to move on to other circumstances. So Paul was able to say, "Whatever I'm doing, and wherever I am, I like it. I like me here. And if God puts me here again tomorrow, I'll like it then, too" (cf. Phil. 3:12-14; 4:11-13).

GOAL-ORIENTED

People with good self-images are very goal-oriented. They have a burning desire to do something with their lives. They know that their lives have meaning and purpose. They continually strive to discover that purpose and to achieve it. They set goals for *every* area of their lives—professional, personal, physical, spiritual, intellectual, and emotional.

One reason why so many people don't like themselves is because, even though their businesses are doing well or everything is going great for them in their careers, their family lives are going to pieces. They are unhappy at home. And instead of admitting that something is wrong and trying to find out how to address it, they get angry and blame themselves, or lash out at their families, only making matters worse. They find fault with those who speak and write about love and the family. By putting down those who espouse the very things they are trying to avoid, they temporarily feel better.

How will you ever get what you want if you don't know what you want? How will you ever achieve all that you ever dreamed of achieving and become all that you were meant to become if you don't set goals to work toward in order to get there? Studies indicate that only about 3 percent of the American people set goals for their lives. This suggests that most of us aim at nothing, and probably end up achieving it!

God wants us to make plans and set goals. All the great men and women whom God has used throughout history have had goals. Moses had a goal to lead the Israelites out of Egyptian bondage. Jesus Christ had a specific goal to do his Father's will. His whole life was lived with that goal in mind. Everything he did and said took him one step closer to the purpose for which he was sent. As early as age twelve, he said that he had to be about his Father's business. And when he hung dying on the cross, the very last words he spoke were, "It is finished." His purpose on earth had been achieved. His goal had been accomplished.

God expects us to use the talents and abilities he's given us so that we may become the kind of people that will bring glory to him. Anything less would be accepting less than God's intended best for us. In our quest to discover who we are, if we float aimlessly about without goals to work toward, we become helpless, frustrated, and bitter. In order to have a good self-image, a person *must* set goals for her life. (I will tell you how to do this in more detail in Part Three.)

EASILY MOTIVATED

People with good self-images are easily motivated. They get excited about almost everything. They want to taste life and try new things, experience other people, and accept new challenges. They are self-motivated. It's almost as if life itself motivates them to live it to its fullest.

When my son was sixteen years old, I recall going down for breakfast one morning, only to discover a certain tension in the air. My son and his mother had been having words.

As I sat down, my wife said, "Lewis, make your son eat his breakfast."

Naturally, I replied, "Son, eat your breakfast."

"Motivate me."

My son's answer indicated disrespect, but he was also telling me something. All of us look to someone or something else to push us and give us that little spark that will set us into motion.

But I have news for you. It doesn't work that way. No one can motivate anyone else. Remember that. What people *can* do, however, is create a climate of motivation—in which a person begins to see herself as she can be, as she has the right to be, as she desires to be, and as she was created to be. As a result, she begins to motivate herself to do the things necessary to get there. You must create a climate of motivation in which those you love can see their own self-value and their own self-worth, in which they can begin to view themselves as winners.

In the Football Hall of Fame hangs a helmet with the following inscription below it: "Bobby Lane never lost a football game. Time just ran out."

A person with a good self-concept is self-motivated and says to himself, "I never lose. I just sometimes don't win." Such people get excited about life. They experience a thrill in competition. They realize that although someone else may win this time, they can win another time. They aren't discouraged by defeat. They don't view defeat as failure, but rather as a stepping stone to the victory ahead.

This outlook helps people to look to the future with confidence instead of with fear and apprehension. Such an outlook helps people to maintain a realistic view of the past as they move on to the better things of today. It also helps people to be more aware of the present and become excited about what today has to offer.

When this attitude is applied to all phases of life, it's easier to enjoy all the things that life has to offer. This attitude creates a climate of self-motivation wherein a person realizes he has a right to succeed, and was created to be a winner if he will only try.

REFUSE TO CARRY GRUDGES

I grew up hearing, "If they get me—boy, I'll get them." I couldn't wait for my turn to "get" somebody. And, yes, I got my turn several times. But later on, I discovered that life is too short, and that we don't hurt anyone but ourselves by carrying grudges around. Psychologists and physicians attest to the fact that old, hidden grudges can physically manifest themselves in such forms as ulcers and migraine headaches, just to mention a few.

Not only is it physically detrimental to carry grudges—it's spiritually detrimental as well. In Matthew 5:22a, Christ admonishes us, "But I . . . tell you that if you are only angry, even in your own home, you are in danger of judgment!" (TLB).

When I first moved to Austin, I was president of an insurance company. I had worked very hard to build that company up and was proud of what it had become. The chairman of the board was an old man who had been extremely good to me. I loved him very much. When he was in his late eighties he became gravely ill; everyone knew it was just a matter of time before he would die.

One day I visited him at his home. We began to reminisce about the early days when the company was struggling, when sometimes we thought we couldn't even open the doors because the company didn't look as though it was going to make it. We talked about one particular time when our stock had gone down to thirty-five cents a share and the future looked bleak. The old man began talking about some friends of ours who at the time had refused to help us out in our time of need. He felt as if we had been attacked.

"I want you to know something, Lewis," he said. "I'm going to get them yet."

As I sat there, looking at this man whose life was ebbing away, I didn't have the courage to tell him that most of these people had been dead for quite some time. But, here he was, nearly ninety years old, still carrying around old grudges that he would probably take with him to his grave.

When a person likes himself, he doesn't take things so personally. He remembers that people usually attack one's performance, not one's person. He also has the capacity to forgive others instead of carrying grudges.

SNAP BACK FROM DEPRESSION

Everyone has periods of depression from time to time. This is normal. But people with healthy self-images don't stay depressed. They snap back from depression and get on with their lives.

I do a lot of traveling, and, consequently, I get tired. Sometimes I have to stay up half the night in order to be in a particular place the next morning. When my head finally hits the pillow in my hotel room, I feel like I'll never get up again. At times like these, I sometimes get depressed and wonder if it's all really worth it.

Then, when I return home and open my mail, something happens to me that snaps me out of it. What I always find is a stack of mail waiting for me from people across the country who have benefited from what I've told them.

I remember one letter in particular from a nine-year-old boy who wanted to share his goals. In his nine-page letter, he proceeded to tell me that he wanted to be the tennis champion of Texas before he was twenty-one years old. That turned me on. Realizing that I had helped this child learn how to set his goals snapped me out of my depression. I realized, once again, that it *is* all really worth it. I just need to be reminded once in a while, like anyone else.

We all get knocked down. We all make mistakes. We all stub our toes. But people with good self-esteem can bounce back from depression; they are able to learn and benefit from their mistakes. This is the message of Romans 8:28: everything is working for good for those who love God and are following his will. We mustn't ignore our mistakes and failures. Rather, we should see the possibilities that are waiting there.

CAPABLE OF DEEP, MEANINGFUL RELATIONSHIPS

Three hundred years before Christ, the Greek philosopher Theophrastus said, "True friends visit us in prosperity only when invited, but in adversity they come without invitation." I believe that nowhere in history is this accurate view of friendship better demonstrated than in the friendship between Gale Sayers and the late Brian Piccolo.

Both running backs for the Chicago Bears football team, Gale and Brian began rooming together in the late sixties. It was a first for race relations in professional football as well as a first for both these men—one black, the other white.

Despite their color difference, these two athletes enjoyed a poignant relationship both on and off the playing field that became something very deep—something so close that words could not describe it. Their special friendship was later portrayed in the Emmy award-winning film, *Brian's Song*.

Their deep friendship was put to the test two years later when cancer cut Brian Piccolo from his team—a severing experience that Gale Sayers shared, because when one hurt, the other felt the pain.

The Professional Football Writers dinner was held shortly before Brian's cancer took his life. Brian and Gale had originally planned to attend the dinner together with their wives. But instead, Brian lay in his hospital bed, alone, but not forgotten.

That evening Gale Sayers received the George Halas Award for the most courageous player in professional football. Hot tears stung his eyes as he remembered his friend, Brian, whom he felt was much more courageous than he.

"You flatter me by giving me this award," Gale said. "But, I must tell you that I accept it for Brian Piccolo, a man of great courage who should receive it instead. I love Brian, and I'd like you to love him. Tonight, when you get down on your knees, please ask God to love him, too."

Friendship is simply love in action—not a conditional or fickle love, but unconditional, consistent, and at times even undeserved.

People with good self-esteem are not afraid to open up and share what's in their hearts. They are capable of lasting, deep, and loving relationships. They don't hold back. They're able to say, "Here's where I hurt, and here's where I'm strong. Accept me for what I am."

People with good self-esteem have close personal friends. If they like themselves, it's easy for them to like others. They find it easy to be themselves around others because they aren't constantly on guard or suspicious of what others want or expect from them.

People with good self-images do not spend their lives trying to live up to what they think others expect of them. They are comfortable with who they are. Hence, there's no need for them to change to suit anyone else. They don't live by the motto that people with low self-esteem live by: "I am not who you think I am. I am not who I think I am. I am who I think you think I am."

As mentioned earlier, you need at least one close friend that you can trust and confide in—that one person who accepts you for who you are. People with healthy self-images can also be friends to others. They can say, "When you stumble and fall, I will like you well enough to stand by you, regardless of what others may think or do."

Also mentioned earlier, people with good self-esteem have good solid marriages. In talking about low self-images, it was stated that the number one cause of divorce is the feeling of inferiority (poor self-esteem) on the part of the wife or husband or both. Partners who don't like themselves grow apart, allowing themselves to be consumed by communication problems, money problems, sexual problems, etc. They stop growing in their marriage because they don't trust, communicate, or share.

A must for good marriages is good self-esteem in both partners. In a related way, the Bible speaks of the two becoming one (Gen. 2:24). A husband and a wife are a unit, a team. And if good self-esteem is present, they can be honest with one another. They can share their feelings openly, without fear of rejection. Because they love themselves enough, they can freely love the other with all his or her imperfections.

Understanding God's plan for marriage involves understanding that your spouse is the other *half* of you, that he or she makes you whole. It means realizing that your spouse can help you understand that you don't have to be something you're not in order to be accepted, in order to find your place in your marriage. You can be wrong sometimes and still be a part of the team. You can even admit to your children that you've been wrong and not fear that they will think any less of you.

I remember one day when my oldest son came home late. He'd made a mistake and I let him know it. "World War III" broke out at our house. I took him to his room and reprimanded him severely. About thirty minutes later, his football coach called me to explain why my son was late. As it turned out, it wasn't my son's fault after all.

I went into his room, sat down on his bed, and said, "I want to apologize to you. I was wrong. Will you forgive me?"

He looked up at me and said, "Dad, for the first time in my life, I feel like I can compete with you. We always thought you and Mom were perfect. We didn't realize that you have feet of clay, too. That makes me feel like I can make it now."

We've been given the wrong picture. We don't have to *be* perfect, because we're *becoming* perfect. People who like themselves have good, solid relationships because they aren't afraid to show that they're human. They like and trust themselves, so it's easy for them to like and trust others.

CAN TAKE A PUT-DOWN AND NOT BE PUT OUT

This goes back to what I discussed in chapter 3 regarding potential vs. performance. People with low self-esteem see criticism as a put-down rather than as commentary on their performance. I used to let criticism of my seminar material and presentations really get me down. That is, until I realized that I had been performing for my audiences, not allowing God to use me for his own purposes.

When I finally decided that it wasn't me speaking in front of those people, but God speaking through me, I stopped worrying about what others thought of me. I could now do what he had given me the power and ability to do. He didn't need me to get his work accomplished, but he could sure use me. As a result, I can now listen to criticism as something potentially helpful. I can also let it roll off my back if I see it as a personal attack.

There will always be those people who are quick to pounce on anything positive that another person may say or accomplish. The difference lies in how that person reacts to these attacks. People with positive self-esteem will simply continue to do their best and not worry about the put-downs that others throw their way.

HAVE SELF-CONFIDENCE

Having self-confidence does not mean that a person is self-centered or egotistical. It only means that a person has confidence in his God-given abilities to do anything that he sets out to do, within the range of those abilities. Many Christians

have problems reconciling the humble spirit Christ has commanded us to have with being self-confident and assertive.

Betty Hassler, writing in the *Home Bible Study Guide,* has
tried to define what she sees as the differences between
humility and self-confidence:

> Perhaps we can get a handle on what humility is by
> deciding what humility is not. There are three false
> stereotypes of humility:
>
> *The "Worm" Complex*—Some people are thought of as
> humble when they actually have a low self-image. Such
> a person (1) refuses compliments, (2) . . . puts himself
> down, (3) . . . is unable to accept gifts or acts of kindness
> from others. . . .
>
> *The "Doormat" Complex*—This viewpoint assumes oth-
> ers should walk on you—take advantage of you. . . .
>
> *The "Lone Ranger" Complex*—Persons with this view-
> point don't want others to find out if they do any good
> thing. . . .
>
> A humble person is not plagued by either conceit or low
> self-esteem. . . . "Humility is seeing yourself in proper
> perspective to God and others." From this definition we
> can identify three characteristics of a humble per-
> son. . . .
>
> He has a proper perspective toward God. Although we
> are awed by God as Creator and Judge, Jesus taught
> us to [call God "Father"]. A proper view of God balances
> reverence of God with the love of God. . . .
>
> He has a proper perspective toward himself. Pride gives
> credit to ourselves for what belongs to God. Pride says,
> "Look what I did," rather than "Look what God did."
> . . . When we rely on God's power to develop our poten-
> tial, we have achieved a proper balance between think-
> ing we are everything and thinking we are nothing. . . .
>
> The third characteristic of a humble person is a proper
> perspective toward others. One pitfall, "thinking of oth-

ers as better than yourself," is just as bad as another pitfall, "thinking of others as worse than yourself."

Pick any area of life: athletic ability, intellect, physical features, talents, etc. You will always be able to find someone who is better than you and someone who is worse. Therefore, to measure yourself by others means you must constantly change your standard of measure.[1]

Self-confidence is simply knowing your talents and resting securely in the fact that you can achieve the goals you set for yourself. It is knowing who you are and what you want out of life, and liking both.

Conceit is a false statement of who you are. Self-acceptance is a realistic measurement of who you are. It includes accepting those qualities which make you proud, as well as those you'd just as soon sweep under the rug.[2]

In order to be all that we were created to be, we must learn to accept ourselves with all our imperfections. Genesis 1:26 states that we were created in the image of God. He made us as he wants us, and he did it for a reason. To reject what and who we are is to reject our Creator. He has given us talents that we can use in the midst of our imperfections.

Your self-image has nothing to do with your potential, but everything to do with your performance. Your self-image has nothing to do with what other people think of you, but everything to do with what you think of yourself. Once you can see yourself as a winner and believe you can be all you were created to be, then you can feel comfortable in any circumstance. *Anyone can be a winner!*

8
THE GOOD NEWS

KAREN WAS BORN with a large nose. She had been teased all her life by insensitive, uncaring people. After she was married she even thought her nose annoyed her husband, in spite of his assurances that he loved and married her for who she was inside. Nevertheless, she had saved enough money from her first job to finally do something about the thing which she had been teased about all her life and which she liked least about herself.

After she had plastic surgery, sporting a new, petite, up-turned nose, looking much better to herself and to others, her whole attitude toward life changed. She liked herself so much better that she became a more outgoing person. She began to enjoy life more because she wasn't embarrassed to go out in public. She became more responsive toward her family and friends; all because she decided to do something about the thing she disliked most about herself.

Not everyone has a physical characteristic like Karen's that they'd like to change. Most of the time self-images are developed by remarks and attitudes, with scars being left on the inside. But there are ways to heal some of the damage that's done.

As mentioned before, the things which make you unique and different, setting you apart and distinguishing you from others, are your abilities, characteristics, emotions, values, talents, attitudes, beliefs, desires, and goals for your life. These things make you special. These are the reasons why most people like or dislike you. These are the things that make you *you*.

A good self-image is a continuous journey through a society filled with negative programming and among insensitive, uncaring people. Many people need to maintain a positive, healthy self-image. The following keys will serve to help you enhance your own self-image as you discover who you are inside.

ELIMINATE SELF-PITY

Quit feeling sorry for yourself. Eighty percent of us aren't even aware of other peoples' troubles because we are so caught up in our own. Or, we see others as responsible for our financial difficulties. Maybe it's a job I don't like or a weight problem. Whatever, nobody seems to care. As a result, much needed energy is wasted in self-pity instead of being redirected toward creative purposes.

God loves me. And if I am part of a loving, caring community of people (including my family), there is no reason for me to feel sorry for myself. Self-pity stands in the way of my being able to get control of my life.

"Today is the first day of the rest of your life." Everything you've experienced and everything you've gone through has been but a preparation for this moment. Feeling sorry for yourself will only prevent you from enjoying life. Rise up out of the ashes of your self-pity and do something positive for yourself. Forget the past. It's over. Work positively to achieve your dreams for the future.

LIST YOUR PERSONAL LIABILITIES

On two separate lists, write out in longhand all the things that you don't like about yourself. It's necessary to write this way because studies show that when a person writes things out in longhand, there is more clarity of thought than when dictation, a typewriter, or another means of transmitting thoughts is used. Eighty-seven percent of all learning comes through the eyes. So, when you look at what you've written, it will take on more of a reality. You will become more motivated to do something about what you've written.

In addition, most people don't know what they don't like about themselves until they sit down and actually write it out on paper. Many dislikes are subconscious. Writing them down helps a person deal with the things that make him feel ill at ease and uncomfortable.

Several years ago we took a survey of women who were college seniors. We found that 95 percent of them didn't like the way they looked. Noted psychologist, author, and speaker Dr. James Dobson reports that the number one concern among young high school girls is beauty, while the number one concern among young high school boys is athletic ability. With this normal focus on self during the teen years, is it any wonder that so many people grow up with low self-esteem?

1. On the first list, write down all the things you don't like but *cannot* change. When you complete this list, pray for the Lord to give you the self-acceptance you need in order to live with these things. Perhaps you have some sort of handicap. Remember that Satan delights in convincing people that they are unworthy, that they're losers, destined for a life of failure. But also remember the promise in John 6:37 that God will never reject anyone.

When you are finished with this list, tear it up and burn it! As you watch this list go up in smoke, resolve never to think about these things again. You're rid of them forever. Get them out of your mind and forget about them. You can't change yesterday or some of the things you were born with, so why let them interfere in your life?

You can't change things you've done or unpleasant things you've experienced. Don't beat yourself down with guilt about something that's over and done with. You may be sorry for some things in your past, but you can't change them. What you *can* change is today and tomorrow. You can start to build a brand new life minus the list that just went up in smoke.

2. Make a second list, writing down all the things you don't like about yourself but *can* change, either now or in the future: excess weight you can lose, crooked teeth you can have straightened, straight hair you can curl, poor attitudes you can work on, broken relationships you can mend, a lack of education you can do something about, etc.

Now set goals and make plans to do something about the things on this list. And remember Philippians 4:13 which says, "for I can do everything God asks me to with the help of Christ who gives me the strength and power" (TLB).

LIST ALL YOUR PERSONAL ASSETS

On a separate sheet of paper make four distinct columns in which you list your assets. List everything you like about yourself.

1. In the first column list all the things you can do well. Include things such as playing football, tennis, basketball, fixing a car, swimming, cooking, sewing, playing the piano or other musical instrument, acting, singing, writing poetry, painting, listening to others, speaking in front of groups, refinishing furniture, etc. List everything you *know* you can do *well*.

2. In the second column list at least ten positive character traits you possess. Perhaps you consider yourself honest, loyal, dependable, trustworthy, organized, etc. Don't be modest! List them all without reservation.

3. In the third column list every recognition you've ever received—every honor, every trophy, every award, every certificate, every accomplishment, every victory. You may want to get your spouse or a close friend to help you with this list.

4. In the fourth column list all your personal assets such as education, work experience, knowledge you've acquired on your own, volunteer work you've done, etc. List anything

that makes you unique and different from others and serves as a personal asset in your life.

God has given all of us talents and abilities to use. Some of them just haven't surfaced yet! You may still be discovering yours. If so, then you'll want to update your lists periodically to reflect these new discoveries.

Once you've completed your lists, keep them in a handy place and read them first thing in the morning every day for the next twenty-one days. Why? Because you've just made a list of all your liabilities and burned it. It's gone. You've forgotten about it. Nature abhors a vacuum. Unless you program something positive into your mind to fill that vacuum— something new and refreshing—your mind is going to start searching for those negative things in order to resurrect them.

It's important that you read the lists the very first thing in the morning. Take your list of assets and tape it to your bathroom mirror. Then, put your alarm clock on the far side of the room so that you *have* to get up and out of bed on the first ring. This way, you won't be able to procrastinate about waking up.

Once you're up, begin your day by reading your list of assets as you get ready for work. Say to yourself, "This is what I am. I must really be one terrific person. I have all this going for me. I can do anything I set my mind to." I guarantee this will change not just your outlook but your whole day as well.

Take a copy of your assets list to work and read it again at lunch. Then read it again before you go to bed at night. Read it three times a day for twenty-one days; you'll begin to get a whole new picture of yourself without having done anything else.

Several years ago, the United States Navy contracted me to teach six thousand Navy recruiters how to sell the Navy to civilians. These men and women had been at sea for approximately fifteen years, on jobs that ranged from electricians, mechanics, and machinists to officers and engineers. I was to make salespersons out of them in two short weeks. The biggest problem I had to overcome was the task of convincing these people who had never sold anything before that they could go out into the heartland of America and convince its young men and women to give up four years of their lives to military service. It was a tall order.

First, we asked them to make the two lists described above. Then, we asked each of them to carry their assets list with them at all times. In addition, once they were actually on the job, they were to carry a list of names of people they had recruited into the Navy. We also had them carry a list of letters they'd received from people who had joined the Navy and had written to express gratitude because they felt they had made a wise decision. Before every sales call, they were to refer to their lists and read them over again and again. In this way, they would condition their minds to believe that if they'd done it once, they could do it again.

Let me use a personal example to illustrate the efficacy of an asset list. I speak before two hundred thousand bright, intelligent, and marvelous people every year. I know that their time is valuable and that they've paid, or their company has paid, for my seminar. I worry that I may not do a good job. Sometimes I get very nervous, and my hands get sweaty. I really want to do a good job for all my clients. I *have* to do a good job. So I carry in my briefcase a folder of letters I've received from clients who've attended my seminars. They have written to tell me what's happened in their lives since. I read these letters before my seminars to encourage me and to help me believe in what I'm doing.

I remember a particular letter I received from a sixteen-year-old girl from Port Arthur, Texas. She had been involved in a tragic accident that left her paralyzed from the waist down. She was a beautiful girl, having been popular in high school and involved in lots of school activities. But the accident had left her, among other things, extremely depressed. Her parents were planning to come and hear me speak, but were afraid to leave her alone. So they brought her with them to my seminar. In her letter she told me that something happened to her at that seminar. She heard things there that made her realize that there was a reason for her being in her wheelchair. And so she decided to go on with her life, putting self-pity behind her. "Something good is going to happen to me," she wrote. "And I'm sending you an invitation to come to Port Arthur to be the speaker at the banquet where I will be crowned the queen of the Gulf Coast Chapter of the Future Farmers of America."

I don't have to tell you that letters like that give me the courage and the strength to continue. They lift me up and make me feel good about myself and what I do. That's why your list of assets is so important. Read it every day.

BE CAREFUL WITH WHOM YOU ASSOCIATE

Dobson terms the following as the "only true values in life": "(1) devotion to God: (2) love for mankind; (3) respect for authority; (4) obedience to divine commandments; (5) self-discipline and self-control; and (6) humbleness of spirit."[1]

Make a list of your own values and beliefs. It's necessary to have a clear picture in your mind of your values and beliefs because they will dictate the direction of your life. You should follow these values when choosing friends and joining groups and organizations.

There's nothing wrong with wanting to belong to a group or a club. Human beings are basically social and seek out others with the same likes and interests. This is only natural. However, it's the *kind* of group you decide to join that's so important. It's a well-known fact that many people tend to follow the values of others, or of the majority, in order to be accepted. Out of fear that others won't accept them for who they are and for the values and priorities they hold, people may end up spending much of their time with losers. Whatever the case, your values must be compatible with those of your friends or you'll experience feelings of guilt and low self-worth later in life.

When you join a club, team, or organization, or when you choose a friend, do so because you share similar interests and values, not because you simply want to belong to something in order to "fit in." This will take courage at times. But, by associating with people who share the same moral values and interests as you, you won't have to be constantly trying to live up to their expectations. Nor will you have to lower yourself to meet their standards, and thus violate all that you know to be right.

The old adage, "You are known by the friends you keep," is true. If you're keeping the wrong company, you will eventually gain the same reputation they have; and their values will begin to influence you as well. You'll eventually experience conflict within yourself because your values and theirs don't mesh.

Sailors know that when they sail downwind, all they have to do is set their sails correctly; the wind does the rest. As the wind fills out the sails, the sailboat glides over the water, gaining its power from a mighty, invisible source.

However, when those same sailors want to return, heading *into* the wind, another scene takes place. The sails must be reset, and the sailors must work much harder. They must take their boat first to the left, and then to the right, leaving a zigzag pattern on the surface of the lake as they laboriously make their way against the powerful wind. It will usually take up to five times as long to return along the same route against the wind as it took to make the original trip with the wind.

The Law of Emotional Gravity says that "one pessimist can pull five optimists down easier than five optimists can lift up one pessimist." That means be careful with whom you associate. Your self-image begins at home, with you, and carries over throughout the day with everyone you meet. So, if you want to be a winner, you've got to associate with winners. Maintain an atmosphere and an attitude of a winner at home, and see to it that it permeates everything you do.

A few years ago, I met the head of the English Institute of Human Studies. I was excited and anxious to meet this gentleman because I'd heard how intelligent he was. I was also eager to ask him a particular question. For years, I'd been trying to find out what Albert Einstein meant when he said, "One incorrect input requires eleven correct inputs to correct."

Now was my chance to get the answer to this burning question. So when we met, I asked this gentleman the meaning of Einstein's statement.

"I don't know," he answered, "but I'll find out."

Two and a half years later, he was speaking before a convention and brought up the question I had asked of him. He said that Einstein meant that five minutes of negative programming requires fifty-five minutes of positive programming to correct. Therefore, be careful with whom you associate.

While on a tour of California's giant Sequoia trees, the guide pointed out the General Sherman—a tree that stands over two hundred feet high and has a seventy-foot circumference. It has stood in California for almost two thousand years. It's awesome. You see, I'm from west Texas where the mesquite trees are about five feet tall and look more like scrubby, overgrown bushes. So, you can understand why I was speechless as I stood there drinking in its majesty.

"I bet the roots on that tree are one hundred feet deep," I remarked to the guide.

"No, sir," he responded. "As a matter of fact, the sequoia tree has roots just barely under the ground."

"That's impossible!" I exclaimed. "I'm a country boy, and I know better than that. If the roots don't grow deep into the earth, strong winds will blow the trees over."

"Not sequoia trees, Mr. Timberlake. They only grow in groves, and their roots intertwine with each other under the surface of the earth. So when the strong winds come they hold each other up."

There's a lesson to be learned here. In a sense, people are like these sequoias. The family, the church body, and groups of friends should be havens where people can come together in love and acceptance. When the strong winds of life blow, these people can serve as reinforcement and encouragement, helping us reaffirm our beliefs and commitments. These should be "places" where people can share their desires, dreams, and goals; where they can strive together to be all that they can be.

Make a rule in your house to begin each morning with every family member working to come to the breakfast table in a good mood. Also, be prepared to share one positive thing that happened to you the day before. Then, each person should share one good thing he has to look forward to that day. The way you begin the day is the way you go through the day. By beginning your day on a positive note, and by beginning your day with winners, you ensure a good day ahead.

READ INSPIRATIONAL BOOKS

I have never met a successful man or woman who wasn't a reader. If you really want to get ahead and take control of your life and destiny, one thing you ought to do is get up thirty minutes early every morning—before the children get up, before the telephone starts ringing, before the radio is turned on—and read informational and inspirational, uplifting material.

Daily reading is another form of positive programming. When you fill your mind with stories about how other people have overcome problems, pressures, and perplexing situations, knocked down roadblocks and obstacles, and surpassed staggering odds, then you can draw from their experiences to muster up the strength and courage to fight your own battles. Reading inspirational material builds within you a reservoir from which you can draw the strength to meet life head-on.

The giant saguaro cactus lives in the arid, barren Arizona desert. It grows to a majestic twenty feet in height and has arms extending in all directions from its trunk, and its roots reach over sixty-five feet into the dry earth below. On the rare occasions when it rains, the roots seek out the water and, through a series of pumps in the root system, actually pump the water up and into the barrel of the cactus above ground. The cactus begins to swell as it makes room to store its life support system. The saguaro cactus can live off the water stored within it for four years. Hence, when the weather is dry and drought comes again, it has a plentiful supply of its vital nourishment.

That's what reading does for you. When things get tough, you have positive information that you can draw from, helping you to find the courage and the strength to go on. I've had people tell me that they don't like to read. They don't see why they should have to do something they don't like to do. I simply respond with, "Do you *like* to get up and go to work every morning?" Sometimes we need to make sacrifices and do those things that are important and that make a difference in our lives.

LISTEN TO INSPIRATIONAL TAPES

Earlier in this book we discussed how you must hear something six times before it becomes fixed in your mind, whereupon you believe it, and act upon it. You can go to a seminar and become motivated to do great things, or read a book and tell yourself you're going to put into practice all it suggests. But if you don't reinforce that information with other material, hearing or reading it six times over, chances are you won't act upon it at all. We know what road is paved with good intentions, and intending to do something doesn't get it done.

Invest in a couple of small portable cassette players. Put one in your car and leave the other one at home. While driving to and from work, back and forth to school, or even in your carpool, listen to tapes that can make a difference in your life.

A study was done at UCLA on the amount of time the average person spends in his or her car. The study revealed that you could have the equivalent of three years of college in only six years if you listened to tapes *only* while in your car. If you are an "average" person, you'll spend twenty-seven hours a year in your car just sitting in front of traffic lights! Why not make those twenty-seven hours count. Listen to tapes instead of watching the guy in the car next to you singing and making a fool of himself. It can make a big difference in your life.

A few years ago I was returning home on a Friday evening after a long week of speeches scattered across the country. I arrived in Austin at 12:15 in the morning—when my flight was supposed to have arrived at 11:40 the night before. My home is about an hour from the airport, so I didn't get to sleep until about 1:30 that morning. To make matters worse, I had to be up two and a half hours later in order to be in Temple, Texas, for a speech at 7:00.

After less than three hours of sleep, I wasn't the happiest

speaker in Texas that morning. I was grumpy and mad at the world. I just wanted to crawl back under the covers and forget the whole thing. Driving to Temple that morning, I even got mad at my employees because they were home sleeping. I felt that if I had to work, they should be working, too. After all, I shouldn't be the only person to be punished.

By the time I reached Georgetown, about fifteen miles north of Austin, I realized that I was about to ruin my whole day. If I did that, I wouldn't be an effective motivator and speaker. So I reached into my briefcase and pulled out my tape recorder, putting on a tape of my *second* favorite speaker, Bob Richards. I'd probably played that same tape about fifty times before, but in the thirty miles from Georgetown to Temple I heard six things on it that were new to me. By the time I got to Temple, I was so excited I could hardly wait to hear myself speak!

You can get a lot more out of listening to tapes than you can out of reading books because you have more *time* to listen to tapes. You can listen in the car, while you're doing housework, while you're taking a bath, etc. And you're more likely to listen to tapes again, whereas, you'll probably only read a book once. Go to your favorite bookstore and buy some good inspirational tapes. Look for such speakers as Bob Richards, Zig Ziglar, Robert Schuller, James Dobson, Chuck Swindoll, and, of course, Lewis Timberlake.

ENGAGE IN POSITIVE SELF-TALK

In chapter 5 we talked about how self-talk can work against us. Psychologists have long known that how we talk to ourselves has a lot to do with our self-esteem. If, when you make a mistake, you repeatedly say, "Oh, I'm so dumb. I can't do anything right," chances are you'll eventually start believing what you say is true.

Instead, you should say, "I need to practice more," or "I need to try harder," or "I need to be more careful the next time. I can do better than that." Self-talk should always be positive. Adults need encouragement just as much as children, and sometimes we must give it to ourselves.

One technique that is widely recommended by psychologists is the mirror technique. Using this technique, a person stands before a mirror and looks directly into her own eyes, repeating the positive thoughts and ideas she wishes to convey.

In his book, *The Magic of Believing,* Claude Bristol describes the power of the eyes. Truly the "windows of the soul," the eyes have a fascinating power that even scientists have failed to explain. But it works! A penetrating gaze into your own eyes will place the positive ideas you wish to convey to yourself deep within your own mind. This works more effectively than reading the same ideas from a book or hearing them from a tape.

Bristol first discovered this technique when he witnessed a drunken friend sober up in less than three minutes by looking at himself in a mirror and emphatically saying, "I am sober." According to Bristol, the drunken friend returned to the party a little flushed, but completely sober.

Whatever the reasons are for why it works, it works. Perhaps it is a form of self-hypnosis. Perhaps there is deeper concentration present when looking directly into the eyes. Regardless of the reasons, it is a powerful way to program your mind positively, helping you to develop a more positive self-image. By using the mirror technique to implant goals and positive ideas into the subconscious, you are that much closer to achieving them.

SET GOALS FOR YOUR LIFE

Get a written, specific goal for your life. Rogers has said that the minute you write down a goal, something happens inside you and you see yourself in a way you've never seen yourself before. Simply by envisioning yourself in better circumstances, you develop an energy and a desire to do the things necessary to get you there.

After a speech in San Antonio, Texas, a young couple came up to me. He said, "Boy, you almost got to me, Mr. Timberlake. You almost convinced me that I'll have to write some goals for my life. My only problem is that I have all these little nagging bills to pay. But once these bills are paid, then I'll write my goals, and I'll be somebody."

"You missed the point," I responded.

I went on to explain to him that if you have a problem, you set goals to overcome that problem, to remove that obstacle, so you can get on with the business of achieving your life's goal. Explaining how they could use goal-setting to pay their bills (which amounted to about $3,000), we agreed on a tentative verbal plan before they left the seminar.

Six weeks later I received a letter from the wife. She told of how her husband had gone home and approached his boss with an idea of how he could earn some extra money. In six weeks he had made $2,000 over and above his regular salary. She enclosed a list of their goals, one of which stated that in the next five years he would have his own Firestone store earning a minimum of $60,000 a year. And I have no doubt that he will.

At the bottom of her letter she wrote, "Thank you. I love you."

A winner is a person who becomes all that God intends for him to become. He's given all of us talents and abilities to use, not abuse. He hasn't given you dreams to dream so he can taunt you. He's placed those dreams in your heart. Psalm 37:4 (TLB) says, "Be delighted with the Lord. Then he will give you all your heart's desires." My favorite Bible teacher tells me that the original Hebrew says it like this, " . . . and he will *place* the desires in your heart." In other words, if you are within God's will, he will give you the dreams and the desires that are best suited to the talent, potential, and ability he's already given you. But what you do with your talent, desires, and things you learn is entirely up to you.

Years ago, there lived an old man who was supposed to be the wisest man of his time. He had never been known to give a wrong answer to any question. He was known to always be able to give a proper answer at the proper time.

One day two young men decided they would try to fool the old man into giving a wrong answer; so they caught a little bird and sought the old man out. Holding the tiny bird in his closed hand, one of the young men said, "Old man, in my hand I have a bird. Is it alive, or is it dead?"

They knew that whatever the old man answered, he'd be wrong. If he said the bird was dead, the young man would simply open his hand and let it fly away. If he said it was alive, he would squeeze the life out of the little bird and again prove the old man wrong. Either way, they would prove themselves wiser than he, thus replacing him as the wisest of men.

The old man stood there in silence, his wise eyes piercing theirs.

Again, the young man said, "Old man, in my hand I have a bird. Is it alive, or is it dead?"

"Son, it is as you will it to be."

In your hand you hold the answer to a successful, rewarding, and happy life. You can squeeze the success and happiness out of it by wallowing in self-pity, refusing to set goals, listening to all that is negative around you, complaining and finding fault with everything and everyone, placing the blame for your mistakes on other people, living in the past, going through life in an atmosphere of fear, doubt, and apprehension.

Or you can bring that success and happiness to reality by opening up to new ideas—by looking at all the assets you possess, setting goals for your life, living by faith and hope for the future, forgetting the past and living for today and tomorrow, and accepting blame and responsibility for your mistakes. "It is as you will it to be." *Anyone can be a winner!*

PART THREE
THE POWER PRINCIPLE

9
"THE MAN I MIGHT HAVE BEEN"

THE OLD MAN had reached the point in his life when he preferred to just sit on his front porch and rock back and forth in the creaky old rocking chair that he'd had since he first married sixty years before. He liked to sit and reflect on his life—on all the things he'd done, all the places he'd been, all the contributions he'd made, the children he'd raised, the wife he'd buried. As he sat and rocked each day, he found it difficult to recall anything significant that he'd done, any footprints he'd left in the sands of his lifetime.

Wanting to know that he'd made some impact in his world, the old man slowly climbed the steep stairs to his dusty attic. There he opened a battered trunk, filled with an accumulation of many years. He began to rummage through all the memories, trying desperately to find one thing that would assure him that his life had been worthwhile.

Buried deep within his trunk, he found an old tattered

journal that he'd kept as a young man. Dusting off the yellow pages, he began to read. His early writings aroused memories of earlier dreams he'd dreamed, of worlds he'd intended to conquer. He remembered how he'd put off his dreams, how he'd waited, and how he'd finally forgotten about them entirely.

Taking a worn, yellow pencil from his pocket, he made one last entry:

> *Across the fields of yesterday*
> *Sometimes comes to me*
> *A little lad just back from play,*
> *The lad I used to be,*
> *And yet he smiles so wistfully*
> *Once he has crept within.*
> *I wonder if he hopes to see*
> *The man I might have been.*

Experts say that the most brilliant person who ever lived was James Crichton, a man born in Scotland in 1560. He finished high school at the age of thirteen and college at fifteen. He had a masters degree by the time he was seventeen years old. When he was nineteen, he traveled all over Europe challenging authorities on his talent and meeting them in open debate. They say that James Crichton could answer any question on any subject in any one of ten different languages.

He was equally adept in all the social graces. He was an expert horseman, an adroit card player, and a graceful dancer. They called him the "Admirable Crichton." Parents held him up as a model and example to their children.

At the age of twenty-two, James Crichton was killed by a drunken prince who had employed him as his tutor. If you should search the history books, you'll find no great works that bear his name, nor any lasting monument to his intellect and his abilities. He was like an inanimate library—able to record everything that passed into him, but unable to produce anything. His only desire in life had been to show the world how brilliant he was. He never *did* anything. He had no goals for his life.

Then there was another young man who lived only thirty-three years.

> He way born in an obscure village. He worked in a carpenter shop until he was thirty. He then became an itinerant preacher. He never held an office. He never had a family or owned a house. He didn't go to college. He had no credentials but himself. Nineteen centuries have come and gone, and today he is the central figure of the human race. All the armies that ever marched, and all the navies that ever sailed, all the parliaments that ever sat, and all the kings that ever reigned have not affected the life of man on this earth as much as that *One Solitary Life*.[1]

Jesus Christ had a reason to live. In John 10:10b Christ said, "My purpose is to give life in all its fullness" (TLB). The whole New Testament speaks of how he came to seek and save the lost. In chapter 7, we spoke of Christ hanging from the cross and saying, "It is finished." His goals had been accomplished.

The greatest tragedy in life is discovering on your deathbed that you've never really lived, that your whole life has been a futile investment in idle activity. Statistics show that by the time Americans reach the age of sixty-five, 95 percent of them are either dependent upon friends, relatives, or charity, or they must continue to work. In the richest land of all, many people die poverty-stricken because they never set any goals for their lives, goals that could have included plans to obtain their dreams; plans that could have lifted them from the pits of where they were to the pinnacles of where they wanted to be.

What separates the average person from the above average person are the things that person *does* with his life. What distinguishes the mediocre from the achievers are the goals they set for their lives. I could write volumes about people who are just like you, who have been in situations like yours, and who suddenly became super achievers because they learned to set goals and work toward them.

Following are seven major reasons why people don't set

goals. Perhaps you'll find yourself or some of your friends in the following descriptions.

WE DON'T KNOW WHAT WE WANT

First of all, the reason most of us never *get* what we want is because we honestly don't *know* what we want. Rogers has said that you can have only one thought in your mind at a time; and that it lasts only from six to eight seconds, and it's gone. Without concentrating on goals and making plans, your dreams are always going to be just that—dreams. The Sears catalogue is commonly referred to as the "wish book." But it ceases to be a "wish book" when a person *does* something about getting what it advertises between its covers.

Earl Nightingale has said that the majority of people who have failed are people who never began. How can you ever get the things you want out of life if you don't know where you're going, and you don't have a plan to get there? Every sensible person who starts out on a long trip takes a road map along. Goals are simply the road maps for your life. And each goal you set and achieve becomes a little town along the way—a step toward your ultimate destination. But if you don't know what you want out of life, it stands to reason that you don't have any goals.

Many Christians think that we shouldn't make plans or set goals because the Bible tells us not to worry about tomorrow. I disagree. Again, Jeremiah 29:11 (TLB) says, "For I know the plans I have for you, says the Lord. They are plans for good and not for evil, to give you a future and a hope." God wants us to make plans.

I could ask *any* given group of people to write down on paper where they plan to be within five years, and 90 percent of them couldn't do it. People spend more time planning their vacations than they do planning their lives. A Harvard University study revealed that only 3 percent have written goals for what they want in life, 7 percent have a fuzzy idea, and 90 percent have no goals at all.

The average college student changes his or her major *four* times before graduation. Ninety-five percent of those who do graduate from college end up in vocations different from that in which they got their degrees. The truth is that most people don't have any idea of what they want out of life.

WE DON'T BELIEVE GOALS WILL WORK

Dr. William James, the father of American psychology, said that your belief at the beginning of any project determines its outcome. If you don't believe something will work, you probably won't try it. This is the second reason why people don't set goals.

I met one of this country's most popular young movie stars on an airplane last year. As we sat talking, he told me about his girl friend and their two children. After years of living together they were finally "thinking" about getting married. But they couldn't get married until their lawyers finished drawing up a prenuptial agreement.

"What do you think about that?" he asked.

"That's the worst thing I've ever heard," I answered.

"Why?"

"Because, you've already conditioned yourself for divorce and failure. You haven't even said 'I do' yet and you're already saying, 'I'm not going to.'"

Deep down in his heart, he has convinced himself that the marriage isn't going to work. That's why he hasn't married her even after two children. It also is why he needs a prenuptial agreement before he does marry her. Your belief at the beginning of any project determines its outcome.

During the Civil War, Admiral David Farragut (best known for his famous line, "Damn the torpedos! Full speed ahead!") gave an order to a young naval lieutenant to take his ship into Charleston Harbor to do battle. The young man took the ship toward the harbor, then turned around and returned without carrying out the order.

With the young lieutenant standing before him, Admiral Farragut reprimanded him. "Why didn't you do as you were ordered?"

"I just couldn't, sir. The wind wasn't right, and I couldn't set my sails."

"No, that's not true," the admiral responded.

"Sir, the water was too choppy, and I couldn't get through."

"That's not true, either."

"Sir, the shell fire was too heavy."

"No, that's not true."

"Then why couldn't I carry out your order, sir?" the young man asked.

Demonstrating his wisdom, the admiral responded, "Because you just didn't believe that you could."

WE CONFUSE ACTIVITY WITH ACCOMPLISHMENT

Most of us have been told that we'll get ahead if we'll just "work hard." So we work, and work, and work, and nothing happens. We don't achieve those dreams that we've dreamed. People don't get ahead simply by working "hard." They get ahead by working "smart."

A French entomologist took a caterpillar and placed it on the rim of a flower pot. Inside the pot he placed pine needles, the caterpillar's favorite food. The caterpillar began to crawl around the rim of the pot, smelling those pine needles, and trying desperately to get closer to them. It crawled around for seven days and seven nights, anxiously trying to get to the food its body needed. One week later it died of starvation. It confused activity with accomplishment. Goals can take you out of the endless circles of activity and point you to the road of accomplishment.

WE CONFUSE WISHES AND WANTS WITH GOALS

If I were to ask a group of people what they wanted out of life, I'm sure I'd get answers such as "I want to be a better husband," "I want to be a better wife," "I want to be a better parent," "I want to go back to college," "I want to buy a bigger house for my family," or "I want to make $60,000 a year."

Most of us have just as many wishes as we have wants: "I wish I could lose some weight," "I wish I looked better," "I wish I had a better life." Someone once said, "If wishes were money, beggars would be kings." A wish, by itself, won't do you any good. It may excite you, but it won't *disturb* you. In other words, a wish or a want will not prompt you to *do* something about it, but a goal will.

My wife and I took a vacation to Switzerland this past year. It was wonderful—just the two of us, away from work and all the stresses and pressures of a daily routine. I *wish* I was back there again sometimes. But I don't wish it enough to do anything about it right now. Thinking about it makes me feel good, but it doesn't disturb me enough to make me take action. A goal, on the other hand, will excite you and disturb you enough to get you to take action in order to satisfy it.

Joseph II lies buried in a tomb in Austria. The following words are inscribed over his tomb's entrance: "Here lies Joseph II, Emperor of Austria. A man with the greatest of intentions who never carried out a single wish in his life."

Wishes can become goals. But goals can never become wishes. We can turn a wish into a goal only when we write it down, develop a plan of action, and then do the things necessary to accomplish it. A wish may interest us, but a goal excites us and forces us to take the necessary steps in order to accomplish it.

WE ARE AFRAID WE'LL FAIL

The fifth reason why people don't set goals has to do with fear.

When it comes to setting goals, people are afraid of two things. First, they're afraid to set goals because, if they fail, they may discover that what they suspect about themselves is true. If they set a goal and fail, they will appear to be failures in the eyes of their families, their friends, and their associates. So why take the risk? This goes back to our discussions on low self-esteem and anticipation of failure. If you haven't corrected, or aren't working on, your self-image, then it can be difficult to visualize yourself as successful, as achieving the goals you've set for yourself.

Second, people are afraid to set goals because they're afraid of success itself. Perhaps their low self-image makes them believe that they can't succeed. Or maybe they are afraid that they can't handle success, or that it may change their life-styles, or their values. Once again, they might be viewed as failures. People who are afraid to set goals go through life allowing fear to run their lives for them.

WE DO THE URGENT AND NOT THE IMPORTANT

Most of you may put this book down after you've read it and tell yourself that now you're really going to write some goals. But this is Sunday afternoon and the Cowboys are playing. And then, of course, tomorrow evening there's "Monday Night Football," and you can't miss that. Tuesday night is PTA, so you can't do it then, either. Wednesday night is the prayer meeting at church. Thursday night is your daughter's band concert. Friday night is your son's soccer game. You've promised to help your friend move on Saturday. Sunday morning there's church, and Sunday afternoon the lawn needs mowing. By the end of the week, you've lost the enthusiasm and excitement you had about setting goals.

I'm not saying that all those things described above aren't important. I am saying that most people tend to do the immediate before they'll even sit down and think about the future.

Goals should be written for every area of a person's life. Children should be taught to write goals for their lives as well. Perhaps your daughter wants to be a professional musician. How can you teach her to write out her goals if you won't write goals for yourself? You must *take* the time to learn about goals. Then, you must *make* the time to write goals out for you and for your family.

WE DON'T UNDERSTAND THE TRUE FUNCTION OF A GOAL

The seventh and final reason why people don't set goals is because they don't realize or understand that the true function of a goal is to produce *power*. Instead of telling your friends that you have a goal for your life, try telling them that you have *power* in your life.

Everyone would like to have power. But most people believe that having power comes *before* the goals. They don't realize it's just the opposite. The goals provide the power you need to become all that you can become. Writing down your goals helps you to envision what you can be, what you can accomplish in your lifetime.

A secretary called me after attending my seminar for Firestone in Austin a few years ago. She told me she enjoyed the seminar except for one thing. She said that I looked directly at her each time I said that a person needed to get a goal for his or her life.

"Let me tell you something," she said. "I don't need a goal for my life. I've got a great life. Things couldn't be better. And I'm going to write you a letter and tell you all about my life to prove to you that I don't need a goal."

"That's wonderful," I said. "I'll look forward to getting your letter."

She wrote me two and a half pages telling me about how wonderful her life was. When I finished reading her letter, I telephoned her.

"I appreciate your letter," I said, "but let me ask you one question that wasn't answered in your letter. Are you happy?"

"Am I what?" she exclaimed.

"Are you happy?"

"What do you mean? How can you ask such a thing?" she shouted before she hung up on me.

About fifteen minutes later, she called back.

"Why would you ask me a question like that?" she inquired softly.

"Well, I read your letter. You said that you get up every morning and go to work; that you work all day at your job, come home in the evening, feed the cat, fix yourself a little supper, watch TV until about 10:00, and then go to bed. I just want to know if you're happy. Is this what you want to do for the rest of your life? Don't you feel there's something missing?"

"Oh, if you only knew," she said. "I'd like to have just a little bit of power to do something different. But, I don't have that."

Power. That's what a goal is. Remember what we discussed in chapter 4 about how the subconscious mind works? You talk to your conscious mind in words, while your subconscious mind works with pictures, with something it can visualize. Once you set a goal and write it down, it becomes fixed in your subconscious which makes it believable. It becomes something you have a right to, something you believe you can achieve. Once you believe something, your mind will go to work and make you act accordingly. If you set a goal, your mind will furnish the power and the will for you to do the things necessary to accomplish that goal.

In 1939 an eight-year-old child ran happily playing baseball in the warm afternoon sunshine. The next morning he was fighting for his life, stricken down by a wicked, crippling virus for which no cure was known. Doctors told his parents that Buddy had polio and, chances were, he would not only never walk again, he might not live through the high fever that accompanied his disease. To his parents, it looked as though success for their young son was out of the question; failure was imminent, and death was lurking around the corner.

Buddy remembers lying in a dreamlike state, hearing the doctors dismiss his young life. At the age of eight, he unknowingly set his first goal, vowing subconsciously that he would beat the polio which had beset him, and go on to live a long and healthy life.

At that time, no one knew of anyone who had ever run a 108-degree fever and lived. But, somehow, to the doctors' amazement, he miraculously recovered. Although he still had his life, Buddy had lost the use of his limbs except for his left arm. Over the next few months, Buddy's mother shed rivers of tears for her young son and his withered body. All the while, he reassured her that someday he would walk and play like every other healthy young child—again unknowingly setting goals for what he wanted to accomplish next in his life; and most importantly, he *believed* that he would indeed reach those goals.

Four months after this courageous declaration, Buddy's mother walked into his room to find him standing shakily beside his bed, holding on with his good left arm. Standing there beaming with pride at what he'd done, Buddy asked his mother for a stationary exercise bicycle so he could try to get back the use of his withered muscles. This nine-year-old child sensed, or perhaps knew, that physical therapy could help him; and by setting yet another goal in a succession of many, he was subconsciously giving himself the power to strive for his dreams.

Strapped onto his exercise bike, Buddy rode more than one hundred thousand actual miles during the next eight years. With every straining push on the pedals, he strengthened his muscles. And they gradually responded to his undying efforts. By the time Buddy began high school in Nederland, Texas, he could walk. However, the circulation in his legs was still so bad that if he tried to run he would collapse on his face. His doctors told him that the only way he could run was on his toes; this would keep the blood pumping through his veins. This method of running was so successful for Buddy that he then decided he was going to play sports! Still another goal.

During his adolescence, Buddy grew into a 6-foot 8-inch, 205-pound giant, inheriting his 6-foot 7-inch grandfather's stature. Undaunted by his immense size, Buddy remained thankful to God that he was alive, healthy, and still able to motivate himself to greater and greater accomplishments each succeeding year.

Because of his great height, Buddy played high school basketball and became an outstanding center during his senior year. Texas A & M University recruited him and thus acquired the tallest player in the history of Texas A & M at the time.

During his years at A & M, Buddy discovered track and field, a program which his small town high school had not offered. He loved to run around the campus track, exercising his legs, and simply enjoying the fresh air and sunshine—

experiences he could never get enough of after his long confinement during his childhood years.

One day, while running the oval track, Buddy spotted some classmates practicing the high jump. Always curious and eager to learn, Buddy asked them to explain the technique. They patiently demonstrated the high jump for him, showing him the beginning takeoff steps, the pushoff, and the final twist necessary to propel a person over the bar.

"Back up, fellas," he said.

Buddy took his position, ran the few necessary steps, and then hurled his immense frame over the bar with ease.

The track coach standing on the sidelines saw what had happened and couldn't believe his eyes.

"Come here, son!" he shouted, excited over his new discovery.

Three years later, well-coached Buddy had become the number one high jumper in the nation. At that time, he calmly announced to his coach that he would win a gold medal for his country when he participated in the 1952 Olympic Games in Helsinki, Finland. He had set another goal for himself.

Officials, coaches, athletes, and fans in Helsinki couldn't believe that anyone who had been jumping for only three years could possibly win any medal, much less a gold. It was simply unheard of. But, they didn't know Buddy; and true to his character, he ignored their skepticism, winning the gold medal by jumping 6 feet 8.32 inches for a new Olympic record. After trying unsuccessfully to increase this record by another inch, Buddy finally admitted that five and a half hours of intense competition had taken its toll on his physical stamina and endurance.

Buddy had spent his entire life setting and achieving seemingly impossible goals for himself. The sense of accomplishment and satisfaction that he realized from those achievements gave him power to go on to even greater things in his life.

When he returned from the Olympic Games, he set still another goal: to break the world record in the high jump, which, at that time, stood at 6 feet 11 inches. As with the four-minute mile, experts said it was impossible. It couldn't be done. But so-called "experts" had scoffed at the Wright Brothers and Thomas Edison; and Buddy, like those far-sighted men, ignored his own critics. This was his personal goal, and he knew that he had the power to accomplish it. He *believed* in himself and in his own abilities, and nothing anyone else said mattered.

When he returned to Texas A & M after the Olympics, he did a strange thing for a 6-foot 8-inch athlete—he enrolled in a ballet class. He felt that he had achieved all that he could by raw, brute strength; it was the ballet class that could give him just the right amount of honing around the rough edges that he needed to propel himself over the high jump bar at near 7 feet. And although many people laughed at him, no one told this 6-foot 8-inch giant that he looked funny in a ballet leotard. Even if they had, Buddy wouldn't have cared. He was working on a specific, personal goal, and he knew what he was doing would be beneficial to his athletic performance.

Several weeks after he began ballet, Buddy jumped 6 feet 11.75 inches and broke the existing world record. On his next try, he cleared 7 feet in front of several witnesses! He was ecstatic. Now he knew that the elusive record was within his grasp. The mythical seven-foot barrier had been broken and could be broken again.

Within five months of the world championship meet in Ohio, Buddy broke the ankle of his right foot. Doctors told him that there was no way he could jump within five months. He must forget his goal. But, again, they didn't know Buddy, or the things he'd accomplished in his lifetime, or the power within him that drove him to pursue his dreams.

"I'm going to break the world record in Ohio," he vowed to himself. Nothing could stop him. Not even a broken ankle.

Five weeks before the meet, Buddy cut off his cast and hobbled onto a basketball court to try out his foot. He limped and plodded up and down the court, trying his wounded ankle first this way and then that, putting pressure on it as he knew he must during a track meet. Going against his doctors' orders, he continued to exercise his foot and use it for the next five weeks.

When the world championship meet took place in Ohio

that year, Buddy was there, pacing the sidelines, nervously awaiting his turn at the high jump bar. His first two attempts caused such intense pain in his ankle and foot that he went through the bar instead of over it. On the third and last possible try that he would ever have to accomplish this goal, Buddy grit his teeth and propelled himself from his unhealed ankle, sailing over the bar at 6 feet 11¾ inches for a new world record. On that day, Walter "Buddy" Davis's name leaped out of obscurity and into the record books forever. He had reached still another in a long series of personal goals.

Buddy's successes didn't end there. He has continued to accomplish new goals—goals that have given him a power he never knew he had before. Today my friend is still pursuing his dreams and still doing things that others say he can't.

A goal is that surge inside that lifts you, pushes you, and forces you to become the kind of person you have the potential to become. It gives you the power to do things you only dreamed of doing before.

Remember what we said in chapter 4 about having a "climate zone"? You are either going to be a thermometer or a thermostat in your lifetime. There's not much to a thermometer—a little glass tube with red or black markings and a small ball of silver mercury on the inside. You can place it in a refrigerator and the mercury will shrink, or you can place it in the sunshine and the mercury will expand. Its only purpose is to reflect the environment that surrounds it. The "goal" here is to remain mediocre, comfortable.

A thermostat, however, is different. It has a standard within it that gives it the power to change its surroundings to reflect that standard. Likewise, a goal gives you the power to affect change. Rather than adapt to your "lot in life" and reflect your surroundings like a thermometer, you can have the power, through your goals, to change your circumstances to reflect your standard (goal). Life becomes a challenge instead of a threat as you realize your power to affect change in the world around you.

You may not be able to control what life hands you, but

you *can* control how you *react* to what life hands you. Resolve today to be a doer, to set goals for your life so that you can have the power to be all that you were created to be. *Anyone can be a winner!*

10
THE POWER TO OVERCOME

A NUMBER OF years ago, Grant Teaff became the head football coach at Baylor University, a private Baptist college in Waco, Texas. Baylor hadn't had a winning season in years, and I wondered if Grant had lost his mind when he accepted a position there.

During the first season Grant was at Baylor, the Bears won five games and lost six. The school thought a revival had broken out! They loved him and were looking forward to the winning season they knew he was going to give them the next year.

As a person, Coach Teaff is a real winner and a believer in all the things I'm sharing with you. By age thirteen he had set a goal to become a major college coach. It was obvious that he believed goal-setting can really work. So it wasn't surprising when he asked every member of his team to write down their goals for the coming year. The next day they filed into their coach's office and gave him their lists of goals.

Among the players that day was one of my son's old high school teammates, Aubrey Schulz. Aubrey had not been an outstanding player in high school; he was just bigger than everyone else, his size accomplishing a lot on the field. And when he got to Baylor, he found that he was no longer the largest man on the team. As a matter of fact, he was a lot smaller than most of the other members of the Bears.

"Here it is, Coach," Aubrey said as he laid down his list of goals.

Coach Teaff picked up the list, read it over, and said, "This is great! You see yourself as a winner, don't you?"

"Yes, sir, Coach. I'm going to be somebody special."

"Yes, I see you are," Coach Teaff replied with a doubtful look on his face. "But, you say here that your number one goal next year is to be the first-string All-Southwest Conference center in football. Is that really your goal?"

"That's my goal, Coach."

"Son, we've got a problem with that goal. For three years now you've been a second string guard. How are you going to become a first string All-Southwest Conference center within one year? Things just don't happen that way."

"Coach, I understand about goals. And I know that if I want it and work hard enough, I can have it. And I want it so bad I can taste it. I've even listed the obstacles I need to overcome before I can achieve that goal."

Aubrey laid a second list of goals before Coach Teaff. The very first thing he listed as an obstacle to his goal was that he wasn't big enough. To play All-Southwest Conference football at center, you've got to weigh at least 230 pounds. Aubrey weighed 210. But he told the coach he'd make it. He'd already planned all that out very carefully.

"All right, if you want it that badly, you'll just have to pay the price for it," Coach Teaff said as he continued to read Aubrey's list of goals. "Your second goal is to be an All-American center?"

"Yes, Coach, I can handle that. I want to be an All-American. I really want it, Coach, and I'm willing to pay the price to get it."

"Your third goal bothers me a bit, Aubrey. It's more unrealistic than the first two. You say that you're going to help Baylor win the Southwest Conference championship this next year!"

"That's right, Coach, we're going to do it. Just talk to the team. We've already made our plans. We've got our minds made up, and nothing can stop us now. We're going to win the conference championship this next year!"

"Be realistic, son," Coach Teaff exclaimed. "We've only won two games so far this year! We've won only one conference game. Baylor hasn't won a conference championship in fifty years. With teams to play such as Texas, Arkansas, SMU, and Texas A & M, how do you think we can win one now?"

"I don't know how, Coach. I just know we're going to win it," Aubrey replied confidently.

"If you guys want it and believe you can do it and are willing to pay the price, then I'm in there with you." Grant was practically convinced that they could do it.

At the end of spring training the following semester, the first-string center for the Baylor Bears was my son's friend, Aubrey. He'd gained one whole pound in two weeks!

Aubrey came back to Austin that summer and got a job in a pizza restaurant, where he ate pizza twice a day. At the end of the summer when he returned to Baylor for pre-season practice, Aubrey weighed 217 pounds. He'd turned his weight into muscle by going to his old high school every night after work and running up and down the steps of the football stadium for forty-five minutes. Then he would go to the weight room and pump iron before going home to bed. At 5:15 the next morning he returned to the weight room to lift weights once more before going back to work.

When the football season began at the end of the summer, Aubrey played his first game against Oklahoma State as the first string center for the Baylor Bears. His number one goal had been accomplished.

Oklahoma State had a 245-pound All-Big Eight Conference defensive nose guard who was a literal terror on the field. Before half-time, Aubrey had inflicted a minor injury on that guard and was benched for the rest of the game. The Bears played Southern Methodist University the third to last game of the season. SMU had a nose guard who weighed a whopping 290 pounds. Aubrey took care of him, too.

When the season ended, Baylor had won the Southwest Conference championship for the first time in fifty years! To hear Texas Baptists talk that year, you would have thought the Millennium had arrived! It was unbelievable. Baylor had not only won a football game, but a conference championship as well. Another goal had been accomplished.

When the All-Southwest Conference teams were announced at the end of the season, Aubrey headed the list as a first-string center. Goal number three accomplished.

Next, there was the Football Writers of America poll. And sure enough, Aubrey's name was there as All-American first-string center. Goal number four accomplished.

On January 1, when Baylor kicked off in the Cotton Bowl against Penn State, playing center, weighing 245 pounds, was Aubrey Schulz, the All-Southwest Conference, All-American, first-string center. The Cotton Bowl was simply icing on the cake.

How'd he do that? God got tired of Baylor losing football games! Right? No, Aubrey simply wrote his goals down so that he could see them in his mind's eye. The picture he saw motivated him and gave him the power to pay the price. He saw himself as a winner and acted like one. And he did what he had to do to bring his goals to fruition. He developed goals that had the power to turn an ordinary person into an extraordinary person. He experienced the six things that a goal can do for you.

GOALS HELP YOU CONCENTRATE ALL YOUR POWER, ENERGY, TALENT

I have a friend who taught psychology for sixteen years at Notre Dame University. Since his "retirement," he has spent his time traveling around the country giving speeches and seminars. I have never heard him speak, but I know that wherever he's speaking, he hangs a large banner across the room that reads *"When was the last time you got goose bumps just thinking about your potential?"*

And so it is with goals. They help you to see yourself as you can and should be.

Raised in orphanages as a child, Bernard Baruch later put himself through school, graduating from The College of the City of New York in 1889. As a member of the New York Stock Exchange, he amassed a great fortune from his wise investments. He served as the economic advisor to seven presidents and held many governmental positions as well. He was known as the "park bench philosopher" because he frequently held conferences on the park benches of New York City and Washington, D.C.

When asked how he managed to rise from such depths to such heights, he responded, "I learned from the magnifying glass."

"What does that mean?"

"I saw the sun's rays fall on everyone. But the magnifying glass captures the sun's rays, harnesses its power, focuses its energy, and brings forth fire."

That's exactly what a goal does. It captures your potential, harnesses your talent, focuses your energy, and brings forth accomplishment.

GOALS GIVE YOU ENTHUSIASM

John Wesley, founder of the Methodists, was a small man, weighing only about 127 pounds. He would rise at five o'clock every morning and ride horseback through the English countryside, seeking out people to hear his message. Some days he would ride up to sixty miles, quite an accomplishment in those days. Midnight would find him still preaching, still energetic and unexhausted.

History tells us that twelve thousand people once heard John Wesley preach. Those twelve thousand came by foot, ox cart, horseback, and carriage. They came all day long to hear the little man who could spark enthusiasm in everyone who heard him.

Once, an excited man was so touched by Wesley's message that he rushed through the crowd, grabbed Wesley, and said,

"Dr. Wesley, you're a phenomenal speaker. Thousands came here today to hear you speak. What's your secret?"

"I don't know, son," he answered. "I just set John Wesley on fire, and people come to see him burn!"

John Wesley had a goal that he worked toward. That goal gave him a contagious enthusiasm that radiated from him as he spoke. He believed in his message, and he had the self-confidence to put it forth.

This is the second thing that a goal can do for you. It can give you an enthusiasm for life that you never had before. It can make you excited about getting up each morning. You look forward to each day and all that it will bring.

If you can't get excited about where you are, you *can* get excited about where you're going. You can't have that kind of excitement without a goal.

I fly tens of thousands of miles every year. You may find it hard to believe, but I *hate* to fly. I hate to pack a suitcase and lug it all over airports. I hate standing in line and waiting for my tickets. I hate sitting in a plane waiting for it to take off, and wondering if it will ever come down again. I hate eating airport food. I hate staying in hotels night after night after night. I hate being away from my family every week.

If I hate all this so much, why do I do it? Because I *love* what I do. And I can't talk to people and share with them as I do unless I do something I don't like to do first. I have to be willing to make a few sacrifices in order to do what I love to do most. And so, it's not flying in airplanes that gets me excited and enthusiastic. Rather, it's knowing what I'll be doing when I reach my destination. That's what keeps me going week after week, month after month, and year after year. Likewise, it's not what you have to do to reach a goal that excites you, but the vision of the goal at the end, the thing that you're working *for*.

People can face anything in life if their goals are out there to keep them going. Goals give you the drive to do the things necessary to get from where you are to where you want to be. But you must be willing to pay the price, whether it's riding on airplanes every day, or studying in a long degree program. It's the end result that counts. And this is where the successful are separated from the unsuccessful. The unsuccessful are those who are not willing to pay the price.

The word enthusiastic comes from the two Greek words "en" and "theos," which literally translated mean "God within." The enthusiasm and exuberance that a person experiences about something that excites and uplifts her can sometimes be difficult to put into words. These two words, "God within," say it all.

The last four letters of enthusiasm stand for *I Am Sold on Myself*. This doesn't mean that you become self-centered and egotistical. It simply means that you can develop a self-confidence in your God-given talents and abilities, refusing to place others above or beneath you. You are being true to the admonition to love your neighbor as yourself. You've accepted yourself and agree with what God has made of you. Also, you are confident that you can do whatever you set out in your heart and mind to do.

GOALS HELP YOU DEVELOP SELF-CONFIDENCE

As you begin to accomplish your goals, one by one, you start seeing yourself as a winner. Achievement helps to build self-confidence. And as you continue to achieve your goals, your self-confidence is strengthened.

Remember what we found in Rogers' research in chapter 8? The very minute a person writes down a goal, he begins to feel better about himself. Just envisioning accomplishment plants the beginning seeds of self-confidence in the subconscious.

Aubrey Schulz was certain that he could achieve his goals even before he began to do the work it took to get him there. When he wrote them down, he could see himself as a first-string center, he could see himself as an All-Southwest Conference and All-American center, and he could see himself in a conference championship game. And as he achieved each goal, one by one, his confidence continued to build. I have no doubt that his self-confidence was at an all-time high when he walked onto the Cotton Bowl field to play on New Year's Day of that year.

GOALS HELP YOU MAKE DECISIONS

According to a report in *Fortune* magazine, 68 percent of us cannot, or for some reason will not, make a decision. Why? I believe it is because we're afraid we'll make the wrong choice. We don't have enough faith in our own convictions to take a chance and decide.

The choices are evident, and therefore the decisions are easier when you set goals for your life. This is because the decisions made are based on those goals. If you know where you're going and what you're seeking, then the decisions you make should be easier, because you'll make them with those goals in mind. Those decisions will be made to help you reach your goals. Thus, the fourth thing a goal can do for you is help you make decisions.

Max Gunther wrote *The Very, Very Rich and How They Got That Way,* a book which contains a series of stories on Americans worth over $150 million. The book didn't turn me on. But I really got excited about his answer to a question I asked him when we met.

"Have you ever put anything together about what really makes these people tick? Have you ever done any research on *why* they've been so successful?"

"Yes," he told me, "they all have three things in common."

He went on to tell me that, first, they all have an average of an eighth-grade education. I immediately liked myself a lot better after he told me that. It confirmed what I've said all along about anyone being able to "make it."

The second characteristic that they share is their philosophy that "there's always a way." When something goes wrong, there's a way to solve the problem. They are self-confident people who aren't afraid of a challenge, and they look at every problem and every situation with a positive attitude.

The final common thread running through this group is that they work only on things that matter. They're goal-oriented. They apply themselves only to those things that will help them achieve their goals in all areas of their lives. They know where they want to go, so they have no problem making decisions.

GOALS HELP YOU RECOGNIZE OPPORTUNITIES

If you are among the 90 percent of Americans who are looking for reasons to fail, you can become one of the 10 percent who are looking for an opportunity to succeed when you first begin to set goals. You begin to see opportunities that you were blind to before. You begin to recognize chances to do things that will help you make your mark in life.

History books say that someone once asked Michelangelo how he could have created his magnificent sculpture of David out of a block of stone.

"It's simple," he answered. "I just looked inside and saw the angel David screaming to get out."

He saw an opportunity where others didn't.

In 1916, Clarence Sanders, the owner of a grocery store, was walking down the street on his way to a cafeteria to have lunch. As he passed the bank, his banker stepped out onto the sidewalk.

"I've been going over your books, Clarence," he said. "It looks to me like you've got about three more months before you're going to be bankrupt. Have a nice lunch!"

Clarence continued down the street to the cafeteria. As he stood in the slow-moving line, an idea occurred to him. If people will line up in a cafeteria to serve themselves, they would probably do the same thing in a grocery store. They could serve themselves, check out more quickly, and get better service overall.

He went back to his grocery and converted it into a self-service store, renaming it "Piggly-Wiggly." Thus was born the first modern-day supermarket. Seven years later in 1923, Clarence Sanders sold his *chain* of stores for $12 million— all because he had recognized an opportunity in a seemingly hopeless situation.

Flip Wilson used to say, "What you see is what you get." In other words, you get what you're looking for. This goes back to the Law of Self-fulfilling Prophecy again: "Be careful of what you expect, because you're probably going to get it." It's only when you recognize opportunity in adversity that you'll be able to grab onto that elusive thing known as success. It's only when you do the things that unsuccessful people won't do, that you can overcome defeat and failure.

If you'll check the history books, you'll find that approximately 95 percent of the world's most important discoveries and inventions were made in times of deepest trouble. For example, in the late fifties, the United States made dozens upon dozens of embarrassing attempts to launch a satellite into space, trying desperately to keep up with the Russian space program. But it wasn't until 1961—when a young, ambitious president, John F. Kennedy, set the goal to place a man on the moon within ten years of his inauguration— that the people in the space program really became serious about what they were doing. John Kennedy recognized an opportunity in the midst of failure, and he successfully passed his vision on to the people who worked for him. And because they made his goal theirs, NASA successfully placed men on the moon in July 1969, eighteen months short of the original ten-year goal!

Around the turn of the century, young Clarence took his girl friend for a summer outing and picnic lunch at a nearby lake. He was dressed in a suit with a high collar. She wore a long dress with about a dozen petticoats and carried a parasol to match. As he rowed laboriously in the hot sun, trying to impress his young lady friend, she relaxed beneath the shade of her parasol, looking very sweet and feminine. The aroma of her jasmine perfume permeated the air. He drank it in as he continued to row. In spite of the hot summer sun and the sweat upon his face, he became hypnotized by her beauty as he watched her smile radiating from under the protection of her parasol.

They finally reached their destination—a small, secluded island in the center of the lake. Clarence dragged the boat onto the rocky shore and then helped her out of the boat so she wouldn't get her feet wet. After he placed all their supplies beneath a spreading shade tree, she began speaking to him in soft whispers. He loved her voice and the soft lips that uttered words as beautiful as music.

"Honey, you forgot the ice cream," she whispered.

"Ice cream," Clarence muttered, finally remembering that they'd planned ice cream for dessert.

He got back into the boat and rowed for what seemed an

eternity until he reached the far shore. He found a grocery store, bought the ice cream, and made his way back across the lake for a second time. He got out of the boat and trudged up the hill to the welcome cool shade of the tree under which his girl friend sat.

She looked at the ice cream, batted long eyelashes over her deep blue eyes, and purred, "Honey, you forgot the chocolate syrup."

"Chocolate syrup."

Love will make a person do strange things. So Clarence got back into the boat, rowed back across the lake, went back to the same grocery store, and bought the chocolate syrup. When he returned to the boat, he once again began to row in the steaming, afternoon sun. He rowed halfway across the lake, and then stopped.

He sat there for the rest of the afternoon, contemplating the blisters on his hands and thinking that there must be a better way. By the end of the afternoon, Clarence Evinrude had invented the outboard motor.

Now before you conclude that I made this story up in order to prove a point, check the history of the Evinrude motor. In the first four months of the advertising campaign for the outboard motor, this exact story was told as the origin of the idea. (By the way, Clarence Evinrude later married the girl he had left stranded on an island for an afternoon.)

Goals enable you to see opportunities that most people don't see.

GOALS HELP YOU OVERCOME DEFEATS, OBSTACLES, AND ROADBLOCKS

I once heard a story told by an old cowboy. All his life he had worked on cattle ranches where winter storms took heavy tolls among the herds. He'd worked in an area of the country where temperatures often dipped quickly below zero, where freezing rains whipped across the prairies, and where howling bitter winds piled swirling snow into enormous drifts.

In this maelstrom of nature's violence, most cattle would

turn their backs to the icy blasts and slowly drift downwind. Wandering until they were stopped by a boundary fence, they would huddle together against the unseen barrier. Standing motionless and helpless against nature's fury, the herd would slowly become covered by snow, eventually dying by the scores.

But the Hereford breed reacted much differently. These cattle would instinctively head toward the windward end of the range. There they would stand shoulder to shoulder with bowed heads, facing the storm's icy onslaught.

"You almost always found the Herefords alive and well," the old cowboy said. "I guess that's the greatest lesson I ever learned on the prairie—just to meet adversity head-on and face life's storms."

What a marvelous lesson! Don't attempt to evade the things that come across your life's path. Every human being must decide again and again, and still again, whether to meet fearsome difficulties head-on or run away. And you can't outrun adversity and life's obstacles. These things are a part of life. But you can learn how to overcome them. You can shift your focus from what can't be done to what can be gained from and accomplished in life. This attitude can turn adversity into opportunity, giving you the hope and determination to find ways to accomplish your goals—those things that keep you coming back from defeat, and which help you overcome the odds to conquer the roadblocks and obstacles in your path. This is the sixth and final thing that a goal can do for you.

A study conducted at UCLA revealed that every great person has had to face total abject failure before becoming great.

- John Milton lost his eyesight before he wrote his most impressive epic poetry, *Paradise Lost*.
- Harry Truman was turned down by West Point, but then went on to become President of the United States.
- Thomas Edison's teacher told his mother that her son was "too dumb to learn." But thanks to Mr. Edison, the modern world enjoys many of the products of his Invention Factory in West Orange, New Jersey.

• Mark Twain survived a life of poverty to become one of this nation's most prolific novelists and best-loved humorists.

• Franklin D. Roosevelt overcame his tragic affliction with polio to become one of the world's greatest leaders.

• After suffering a paralytic stroke, Louis Pasteur discovered the revolutionary process of pasteurization.

• Admiral Byrd endured overwhelmingly oppressive loneliness to become an acclaimed explorer.

• When George Frederick Handel wrote the words and music to his beloved *Messiah*, he was paralyzed and threatened with debtors' prison. Today, his beautiful music gives pleasure to all who hear it each year during the Christmas season.

• My favorite example is one of a not so well-known young man whom I first heard about in 1978. This young long-distance runner ran thirty marathons that year totaling 787.5 miles. That may not seem like a very great accomplishment; but it was a tremendous achievement for this athlete who was born with no feet.

These people are not exceptions. They were or are people just like you and me. What distinguishes them is that they refused to be held down by their circumstances or by despair. They were willing to do the things that unsuccessful people won't do. They were motivated to do what they did in order to be all that they could be. And they did it without hurting others and without compromising their convictions and beliefs in the process. A person with a goal has something which gives him the courage to climb out of the pit of darkness and keep going.

One doesn't have to have a physical handicap or disappointing circumstances to be discouraged by what life "dishes out." What makes all the difference is how you react to each situation. Do you give up and moan? Or do you get up and *do something* to overcome your obstacles?

Every person who reads this book will someday face his own "Gethsemane"—a period of questioning whether or not life is worth living. Is the promise worth the price? These are times when the glow burns low, when zeal fades, when doubt flashes its frigid face across our winter path, when tears rush quickly to the eyes. This is the time when life seems its toughest.

We all face times in life when things get so tough that we want to give up and quit. Remember this: *LOSERS QUIT!* A winner will find something good in defeat. He will learn from it; then he will put it behind him and keep going. Anyone can quit. That's the easiest road to take. But life rewards the people who persevere. These are the people with goals— people who have a direction for their lives. It is this direction which sets them apart as examples to a weary, wanting, and dying world.

A young military man came back from the Boer Wars as the greatest hero England had ever known. Everywhere he went he was honored. People flocked from all over the countryside to see him. He later became a leader in civic service, and before he was forty-two years old was appointed Minister to the Navy.

Not one year into his tour of duty, he committed a colossal military blunder. Consequently, he joined the ranks of the rejected, the unknown, and the forgotten. If he had died at the age of sixty-four, history would have held his name as a mere footnote in the sands of time.

When he was sixty-five the king called him back into service. Within five short years, Winston Churchill's name again became a household word. He climbed from the pit of despair to the heights of adulation. Why? The answer lies on a piece of paper that he carried in his wallet. On it he'd written, "I shall study, and I shall learn, and one day my time will come."

Churchill's father had been a political failure. And as a result, young Winston became obsessed with a dream that he would not die a failure, too. He wrote his goal down and lived up to its promise. When he had survived the years of humiliation and failure, he finally became all he had dreamed of becoming. He overcame defeat by keeping that goal in sight.

In his old age, after all his victories and accomplishments, Winston Churchill received an invitation from Eton College to come and speak. When he arrived on that historic campus, lined with ivy-covered buildings, he looked into the freshly scrubbed faces of young men dressed in their suits and ties who were eagerly anticipating his words of wisdom. He knew they were waiting for him to point them in the direction of success, explaining how they could make a mark in their world.

Carrying his Boer hat in one hand and using a cane with the other, Mr. Churchill walked slowly out onto the stage, his famous cigar protruding from his mouth. He hobbled up to the podium, placed his hat and cane on a chair beside it, and looked out at the sea of students awaiting his words.

With that familiar scowl on his face, and his cigar clenched between his teeth, Winston Churchill exclaimed, "Never, never, never, never, never, never give up!" Then he turned and walked off the stage.

That's what a goal will do for you. It will help you concentrate all your power, energy, talents, and efforts on an end result about which you're excited and enthusiastic. That end result will give you the strength and the courage to persevere when the going gets rough. It will help build your self-confidence, giving you a sense of personal achievement and self-fulfillment. It is the road map that you follow to get to your destination of becoming all that you were created to be. *Anyone can be a winner!*

11
FROM DREAMS TO REALITY

WHEN I WAS a young man, I didn't have a goal to become a professional speaker. I wanted to be the world's greatest shortstop. In fact, by the time I turned twenty-one, I had already signed a pro baseball contract. My dream was coming true. There was no doubt in my mind that I was on my way to fame and fortune.

Then during my last Army baseball game I was hit by a pitched ball. The pitcher could throw a ball through a car wash so fast it wouldn't even get wet. The next thing I remember was realizing that my dreams for a professional career were no more.

The only thing that kept me going was the birth of our first child, a son. I then decided that *he* would become the world's greatest shortstop! Before he could walk, I already had a baseball bat and glove in his hand. As he grew, I could see that he was built like an athlete—he moved like an athlete and was strong and well coordinated. I couldn't wait to get him onto a baseball diamond.

When we moved to Austin, I signed him up for Little League, Pony League, and Colt League. He played like a superstar. I started inking up all my pens, getting them ready for the signing of the contracts. This was it! The Austin Pony/Colt Leagues and high schools had sent many outstanding players to the major leagues over the years, and now *my son* was going to go, too. I knew it as well as I knew my own name.

During his junior year, his baseball coach called me and told me he wanted to talk with me about my son. "That boy really loves you, Mr. Timberlake, and he'd do anything for you."

"Well, I love him, and I'd do anything for him, too," I replied.

"Brad wants to quit baseball, Mr. Timberlake."

"No, he doesn't, Coach," I replied confidently. "There must be a misunderstanding somewhere. My boy would never quit baseball."

"I've talked to him, Mr. Timberlake," the coach continued. "I really think we should sit down and talk about this. You see, he really wants to play football."

"Well, he can play football if he wants," I replied. "I don't mind that. But I know he also wants to play baseball. I know my son, and I know what he wants. Brad and I have discussed this many times. He really loves baseball."

I made the coach a promise that I'd talk to Brad. I also assured him that my son would be back out on the diamond for practice the next day.

But, before he hung up the phone, he asked, "Mr. Timberlake, do you want Brad to be Brad Timberlake, or do you want him to be Lewis Timberlake, Jr.?"

Boy, that was a dirty question! But I learned a great lesson that day. I realized that in order to become the kind of father, husband, and boss I wanted to be, I had to create a supportive climate for those who love me and work with me—a climate wherein they could discover who they are and what they want to be, not what *I* want them to be.

If you're going to set achievable goals for yourself, as well as help your loved ones learn how to set goals, you must first understand the elements of a goal—those requirements that make a goal a goal and not a wish or a dream.

GOALS MUST BE PERSONAL

I learned the hard way that you can't set goals for anyone but yourself. Goals must be personal. They must be yours and yours alone. As parents, you can help your children discover their talents and abilities. Doing this will help them have a better understanding of what they can do in life before they set their goals. You can even direct them in *how* to set their goals. But parents can't write goals for their children any more than friends can write goals for friends, colleagues for colleagues, husbands for wives, etc.

Don Fearheiley writes in the *Home Bible Study Guide* that "we can't fulfill our potential by living through others, watching what others do while denying our own ambitions and desires and goals."[1] Setting goals for personal gain is not being materialistic and selfish. It's using the talents and abilities that God has given us in order that we may become all that he created us to be. It's an expression of selfhood, and "Unless we focus on that selfhood we are in effect betraying the purpose God had when he created us."[2] God has a plan for each of our lives—a plan that includes personal growth and development as individuals.

But, even as individuals, our personal goals usually fit into corporate goals—for a family, a church, a business, etc. Therefore, it's necessary to sit down as a family, or as a corporate group, and discuss individual goals in order to see how they do or don't fit in with the family or business goals as a whole. There should be corporate discussion on how the group's goals reflect individual goals and how they all work together for the good of everyone. But, the key here is that an individual's goals must be personal.

GOALS MUST BE WRITTEN

Years ago, one of the great professional speakers of our time spoke on goal-setting at a major eastern university. After his speech, a group of the school's intellectual "elite" decided that what this speaker told them about goal-setting wasn't true. And to prove him wrong, they surveyed that year's senior class. They discovered that only 3 percent of them had written goals for their lives, 7 percent had a fuzzy idea of a goal, and 90 percent had no goals at all.

For ten years they kept track of this group of seniors, ten years later conducting another survey. The results? The 3 percent with written goals for their lives had achieved more than the other 97 percent put together! That group of intellectual "elite" people determined that there must be something to written, specific goals after all.

You will never have goals until you put them down on paper. In chapter 8, we referred to this. Rogers said that something happens in the subconscious mind that urges us to act when we *see* our goals written out in longhand. Also, previously mentioned, you can't dictate them into a machine, you can't type them on a typewriter, and you can't just wish for them in your mind. You have to write them out personally in your own handwriting.

In addition to helping activate your subconscious, writing down goals commits you to them in a way that "wishing" you could do this or that can't. And that commitment urges you to *do something* about reaching your goal or goals. Psychologists say that because of this phenomenon, people who write their goals down have a better chance of accomplishing them than people who do not.

Henry David Thoreau once said that most people lead lives of quiet desperation—something is missing in their lives, but they don't know what it is. They search unhappily, trying to fill that void. But they never find it, because they don't know what they're looking for.

One evening I received a phone call from a young woman who had attended a Sunday school class that I'd taught at my church. After nineteen years of marriage, her husband had left her for a younger woman. She wanted me to talk to him.

"I can't call him," I told her. "But, if he'll call me, I'll talk to him."

A few days later her husband called me. When I asked why he'd left his wife, he told me he didn't know.

"There's just something missing," he said.

"What is it that's missing?" I asked.

"I don't know," he replied.

"Well, what do you want out of life?" I asked.

Again, he replied, "I don't know."

I will never forget a quote I read in *Mad Magazine* that has helped me realize the power of setting goals: "I don't know what I want in life, but I'm quite sure it ain't what I got!"

How can you ever *get* what you want out of life if you don't *know* what you want? Your goals must be thought out, written down, and acted upon. Otherwise, they're meaningless.

Sit down with a pencil and paper. Start writing things down that you'd like to do, things you'd like to have, things you'd like to improve, etc. Your subconscious will start working for you, and you'll write things down you haven't thought of in years.

I have a friend who attended a weekend marriage retreat with her husband. One of the exercises she had to do was to write down personal things that she didn't like about herself, but which she could work to improve. She thought of two to three things right away and figured her list would be rather short. Before she finished writing, she had twenty-one items on her list! Ideas were popping into her mind so quickly that she couldn't write fast enough. The more she wrote, the more things she thought of.

GOAL-SETTING MUST BE CONTINUAL

When I met Milton Berle in Palm Springs, California, I discovered some amazing things about this brilliant comedian. He is the president of the American Longevity Association. And he plans to spend the rest of his life helping people understand that they don't retire *from* a job, they simply retire *to* something else. Retirement is merely a time in life when one's goals must be revised and adjusted to meet the needs of a new situation.

We've been taught that we must get a lifetime goal, and then spend the rest of our lives working toward it. A few people will accomplish their goals, but most will never reach theirs. The challenge is supposed to be in the quest. That's terrible!

You should have a series of goals that will meet your needs and desires for each particular phase of your life. Events, circumstances, and situations change. And if your goals can't change as well, then you are bound to become frustrated and discouraged. Why? Because you haven't adjusted your goals to reflect the changes in your life. As a result, you no longer have direction.

Dr. Abraham Maslow has said that he found when a person completes approximately 75 percent of the steps necessary to accomplish a specific goal, a brand new goal appears. Life should be a series of goals, of growing experiences. Also, goal-setting should be a continual, never-ending process in one's life. The minute you cease to live *for* something, you begin to die.

I never had plans to be a professional speaker. I have a speech impediment slurring certain words that are difficult for me to pronounce. Because I knew that athletes never have to talk, I chose to become a professional athlete. But, when I was injured and had to find a new profession, the best job I could find was as a credit manager for Goodyear Tire in my hometown. After a few days, my boss told me that if I was going to be meeting the public, I had to learn to talk. So, he suggested that I join the Stamford Jaycees. I thought that sounded simple enough, so I did as he suggested.

The president of the Stamford Jaycees introduced me at the next meeting, having asked me to tell the group something about myself. I was so terrified I couldn't even say my name. I almost died! I stammered, turned red in the face, and lost my train of thought. I vowed that if I ever got out of that meeting, those men would never see Lewis Timberlake again.

The main speaker that evening was the vice-president of

the General Telephone Company in San Angelo, Texas. I watched him speak with ease and confidence. I liked the way he sounded, the way he looked, the way he had rapport with the audience. I decided that I wanted to be just like him. So after his speech, I asked him what I could do to be able to speak as he did.

"Run for the presidency of the Stamford Jaycees," he answered.

"I can do that," I responded.

When I became president of the Stamford Jaycees, my friend from General Telephone called to ask if I'd run for the vice-presidency of the Texas Jaycees. His first advice had been pretty good. So I again did as he suggested—and I won. The next year he called and asked me to run for the presidency of the Texas Jaycees, which I also did—and won. He later asked me to run for the vice-presidency of the U. S. Jaycees.

When I won that office, he called me again and said, "Welcome to the world of professional speaking!"

There were years when I never even dreamed that I'd be able to talk in public, much less speak before audiences and eventually make a living at it. But as I accomplished each goal, a new goal appeared and gave me new direction in my life. Goal-setting must be an ongoing, continual process. And every time you achieve one goal, God gives you the ability and the grace to work toward another.

George N. Pierce, chairman of the board of Pierce Arrow, introduced his Pierce Arrow car in 1901. The car soon won a reputation for reliability on the rough and often muddy roads prevalent at the time. After enjoying this reputation for a few years, Mr. Pierce said that his company had made the greatest car ever possible, and that no improvements could be made on it. We now know that the Pierce Arrow is no longer manufactured, because the leadership of the company didn't have the foresight to revise and adjust their goals. They saw nothing more to be accomplished.

On the other hand, the great Italian artist Raphael (Raffaello Sanzio, 1483-1520), when asked which of his paintings was his greatest, responded, "My next one!"

171

What a great attitude! What you become in life is determined by your attitude and by the goals you set for yourself—goals for which you are willing to strive.

GOALS MUST BE ALL-ENCOMPASSING

Goals in one area of your life must be compatible and complementary with goals in other areas of your life. You cannot sacrifice your family on the altar of your work. Your work is only one-sixth of your life, and in order to live a fulfilling and meaningful life, you must not only know yourself in all areas, but you must set goals in the other areas of your life as well.

No one is a one-sided being. We do more than just work for a living. In addition to their work, most people have families, social and spiritual lives, and physical and intellectual activities. No one has ever been born forty years old and working. Although, my children used to think I was! There are other things in your life that make you the unique and special person you are. I suggest you set goals in the following six areas.

1. *Professional/Financial Goals.* This is your calling and your purpose in life. This is the reason you get up every morning at 6:00 and drive fifteen miles in sleet and rain to a cold office. This is what puts food on the table, clothes on your back, and shelter over your head. Most people want to get three things out of their professional lives:

a. *Position.* This implies that a person wants some control, power, and input into how his job gets done. It also implies that along with position comes more money.

b. *Prestige.* This simply means that we want other people to like us, to feel good about us, and to respect us for the accomplishments we've experienced.

c. *Prosperity.* Prosperity usually follows position and prestige. The Bible says it's the *love* of money that is the root of all evil, not money in and of itself (cf. 1 Tim. 6:10). It's when we place making money above all else in our lives that our priorities and our relationships suffer. We work for what money will do for us. We work for food, clothing, shelter, homes, cars, education for our children, vacations, etc. Anyone can have one, two, or all three of these things. But how can a person ever achieve position, prestige, and prosperity if she doesn't know what she wants in her professional life? It's important to set and work toward goals in the professional area of your life.

Professional goals are almost always logical. A person can explain his professional goals in terms of position, prestige, or income. Concerning one's profession, emotions seldom, if ever, enter into the goal-setting process.

As you sit down to write your professional/financial goals, ask yourself the following questions:

- Do I really like the work I do?
- Is there something I would like better? What?
- How can my present work get me to a position or a job that I would like more?
- Do I know the goals of my company?
- Do I really understand my job in relation to my company's goals?
- Do I know what I would do with more money?
- Do I know what I can do for my company in order to make more money?
- Do I have a written plan to make more money?

2. *Family Goals.* Family goals are almost always emotional. Anytime logic comes up against emotion, emotion usually wins. That's why when people can't emotionally justify the sacrifice they must make in a particular job, they suddenly quit and find new careers.

Studies reveal that average parents spend only twenty minutes a day communicating with their children. And nine of those minutes are spent in disciplinary situations. Why is this? Parents make no *plans* to talk to their children. Time is not set aside for family conversations. It's no wonder there's so much rebellion, lack of communication, and misunderstanding among family members. It takes effort that some parents aren't willing to put forth. If you want your marriage and family life to work and be happy, you must work at it.

In setting family goals, you must decide exactly what kind of family life you want. What kind of home do you want to live in? What kind of car do you want to drive? What kind of relationships do you want within your family? Where do you want to spend your vacations? What kind of values do you want to pass on to your children? All these questions can be answered in your list of goals for the family.

A husband can have his individual goals, a wife can have her individual goals, and each child can have his or her individual goals. But, when they come together as a family, there must be goals there as well. And, as I said before, all personal goals must be compatible with the corporate goals of the family.

My wife and I are both from small Texas towns. When we got married we were *poor*. But, like all young married couples, we had great dreams of what we wanted to accomplish in life. We planned our "dream house" and our "dream vacation." But, I knew that if I were going to provide all this for my wife and family, I would have to work hard to make some money. I soon learned that to make that kind of money, I had to pay a certain price. My family goals were tied to my professional goals with a steel padlock. I couldn't have one without the other.

This is why it's so important to sit down and work out family goals *together*. Otherwise, certain members of the family may not understand why such sacrifices are being made. When decisions are made as a family, family members can help each other carry the burden.

Children may honor their parents when they're young, but they will evaluate them when they become older. A time will come when parents will look back and know whether or not they accomplished those things which God allowed them to dream and hope for.

As you sit down with your family to write out your goals, ask yourself and each other the following questions:

- Is my family *really* important to me?
- How often do I tell them that I love them?
- Do I make my time with them "quality" time or "quantity" time?
- How well do I listen to each family member?
- Have I discussed my personal goals with them?
- Have we discussed *their* personal goals?

- Do we plan family nights?
- Do we take family vacations?
- Do we do things together that will strengthen us every day?

3. *Mental/Intellectual Goals*. I once heard Dr. Adrian Rogers speak about how God gives light to light. I understood him to mean that, the more you know, the more God lets you know. Conversely, the more you refuse to learn, the darker it gets for you intellectually.

Printed knowledge is growing today at a rate of five hundred thousand pages per day. All the knowledge available at the time of Christ's death could be placed in one printed volume. That knowledge didn't double until the year 1750—1,717 years later. It took only 150 years (1900) for that knowledge to double again. It doubled again a mere fifty years later (1950), again in ten years (1960), and again in five years (1965). Today, accumulated knowledge doubles every 2.5 years. Experts predict that by the year 1990, knowledge will double every 3.5 *months!*

I read a recent survey which revealed that if a person reads only one book per month, he is in the top 1 percent of the intellectuals in America. One book a month (and *TV Guide* doesn't count!) is all it takes to become a part of this country's intellectual elite. What this tells me is that less than 1 percent of the people in this country are working and contributing to the tremendous knowledge explosion referred to above. Think of the progress that could be made if more people made it their business to be "in the know" and keep learning. Parents are already feeling left behind as their children learn to use computers in elementary classrooms. If we don't want to be left in "the dark ages," we must find a way to improve our intellects.

"Trivial Pursuit,"[3] a game that's sweeping the country, was listed as one of the top five best-selling items during the 1984 Christmas season. Curiously, one of the reasons for its popularity is the fact that it forces people to *think*. It's not just a mindless, pointless way of passing the time. Americans don't normally pursue any kind of intellectual activity once they've graduated from high school or college. It is therefore necessary that we set mental/intellectual goals for our lives.

As you sit down to write your mental/intellectual goals, ask yourself the following questions:

- Do I ever spend time just thinking about me and my life?
- Do I worry needlessly? Is it a habit?
- Am I continuing my education, formal or otherwise?
- Am I keeping up with the latest developments in my industry/profession?
- Do I have a program for "skills" development?
- Do I consistently read inspirational literature?
- Do I use my spare time to listen to inspirational and educational tapes?

4. *Physical Goals*. What are your goals for your physical health? How do you plan to handle stress—the wear and tear of daily living? How do you plan to stay healthy and whole for yourself and your family?

If you could spend just fifteen minutes a day in some physical activity, whether it be a hobby, a sport, or daily exercise, it could totally change your physical fitness. In fact, if you run just one block a night, you're potentially in the top 1 percent of the physically fit in America. For me, it's hard to exercise daily because I'm at that stage in life when I think an active evening is sitting at home watching my left foot go to sleep. But you've heard that modern cliche, "No pain, no gain." It's true.

We must learn to take care of ourselves and preserve our health as best we can. The number one sign of heart trouble is sudden death, because 40 percent of the time there's no advance warning for a heart attack. Daily exercise strengthens the heart, lungs, and cardiovascular system. It's also insurance for good health in days and years to come.

As you sit down to write your physical goals, ask yourself the following questions:

- How well do I take care of my physical needs? Diet? Exercise? Sleep? Dental checkups? Regular physical checkups?
- Do I get enough real relaxation?
- Is there anything I could be doing now to preserve and/or improve my health?

5. *Social Goals*. Surveys say that 70 percent of Americans

are suffering from an acute case of loneliness. People get up in the morning, shower, have breakfast, go to work, come home, eat dinner, watch TV, and then go to bed. They have no social goals, much less social lives.

I know, most people will say they just don't have *time* for anything outside work and home. I must emphasize here that *time is a priority*. You'll never have any more time than you do right now. So, what you must do is learn how to manage your time better. If you want to have more time for social activities, go to your local bookstore and buy a good book on time management.

A good friend of mine was fortunate enough to get a job with one of the largest companies in this country. His first week on the job, he got up at 7:00 in the morning and worked until 7:00 each evening. He brought home two briefcases full of work. As he came in the door he'd kiss his wife, pat his son on the head, and then disappear into his den to work until dinner. After dinner, he'd go back into his den and work until he went to bed.

This routine continued for five weeks. At the end of the fifth week, his eight-year-old son asked his mother why his dad never played with him. He asked her why he never saw his dad anymore. He missed his father. He asked her why his dad had to work all the time, and why he couldn't take him to ball games and movies like his friends' fathers did.

"I don't know, son," his mother answered. "Daddy just can't seem to get all his work done at the office. And so, he has to bring it home with him to finish at night."

Looking up at his mother with deep concern in his eyes, the little boy asked, "Then why don't they put him in a slower group?"

People need time to spend time with their families, to cultivate their friendships, and to become involved in community activities. People are naturally social beings. Without that outside contact, both emotional and physical health will suffer.

As you sit down to write your social goals for your life, ask yourself the following questions:

- Do I really like people?
- Am I afraid to show my feelings toward others?

- Would I like me as a friend?
- Do I talk too much?
- Am I a good listener?
- Do I look for the good in people?
- Do I try to bring out the best in others?
- Am I currently involved in my community?

6. *Spiritual Goals.* Humans, by their very nature, are goal-seeking beings. They are constantly striving to find answers, searching for that something they feel is missing, that something that will bring satisfaction and meaning to their lives. There's a hunger within us that asks, "Who am I?" "Where did I come from?" "What's my purpose on this earth?" Some people have already discovered the answers to these questions. But, everyone, regardless of how religious, needs to set spiritual goals.

For those who believe in God, there is a great need to understand what it is he is calling us to do. Knowing God's will for our lives is what gives our lives meaning and a basis for action in the world. The greatest thrill anyone can have is to come to an understanding of God's purpose for his life. But in order for this purpose to take root, a person must set spiritual goals.

As you sit down to make your list of spiritual goals, ask yourself the following questions:

- Do I believe in God?
- How important is my faith?
- Do I understand my beliefs and convictions?
- Am I doing anything to increase my understanding and beliefs?
- Do my family and friends see spiritual strength in me?
- Is there something I should do to help others?

HOW DO YOU RATE?

On a sheet of paper, draw a circle like the one below. Then divide it up with three straight lines which will give you six separate sections. Label each section for the six areas we have just discussed: professional/financial, family, physical, mental/intellectual, social, and spiritual. Rate yourself on a scale of 1 (low) to 10 (high), according to where you think you are today in each area. A score of 1 should fall in the center of the circle, while a 10 should fall directly on the outside line, or circumference, of the circle. Record your scores with dot markings.

If you have exactly what you want in your profession—the highest position you'll ever want and the most money you feel you can ever make—and you're happy, then you should rank 10 in that area. If you feel you're just starting out and have a lot of growth ahead of you, then you'll probably rank between a 1 and 5.

Do this for all six areas. When you're finished scoring, take a pen and connect the dots; then color in the inside portion of the circle. This should give you a pretty good picture of your life, showing the areas where you need the most work, where you need to set goals for improvement right away. If this picture isn't what you would like it to be, maybe it's because you don't know what you want in a particular area. In that case, you need to explore your heart, your priorities, and your dreams and desires. Next, set goals to bring this area to the point you'd like it to be.

GOALS MUST BE COMPATIBLE

I cannot have a goal for my financial life that conflicts with my goals for my family life. I'm not willing to pay that price. And so, as was stated above, goals must be all-encompassing.

My wife, Georgia Ann, had a dream to become an artist. She was and is very talented. But we both felt that one of us needed to stay home with the children. So, we took a vote and she remained in the home. Now, after thirty years of marriage, we have an "empty nest" again, and Georgia Ann is finally fulfilling her dream by taking art lessons and painting again. Now her personal goals are compatible with the family goals, when they weren't thirty years ago.

The goals in all areas of your life must be compatible. However, remember that they can change as your life situations change. That's why it's necessary to write down *all* your goals, discuss them as a family, and then periodically update those same goals as your circumstances change.

GOALS MUST BE REALISTIC

In setting goals, remember that they must be realistic. A public school teacher making $15,000 a year shouldn't set a goal to become a millionaire by the time he's thirty years old. It's simply not realistic (unless he knows something I don't know). I'm not saying that he can never become a millionaire. I'm saying that he'll never do it on a teacher's salary. If becoming a millionaire by the time he's thirty is really a goal for that teacher, then he needs to seriously consider changing careers. Otherwise, his professional and financial goals will remain incompatible.

Earlier in this book, I stated that you cannot lie to yourself. If you honestly don't believe you have the right, ability, talent, or capacity to achieve a particular goal, then you won't pay the price to get it. If you had asked me twenty years ago whether or not I would ever be a professional speaker, I would have laughed at you, because it wasn't a realistic goal to me then. Twenty years ago, I honestly didn't believe that I could ever do what I do today—no matter what Dr. Norman Vincent Peale or Zig Ziglar said. If you don't believe in something, to you it just isn't true.

Christ says in Mark 9:23, "Anything is possible if you have faith." It wasn't until I had grown and developed in my professional career and suddenly found myself serving as the vice-president of the U. S. Jaycees, that I ever thought such a possibility existed. It just wasn't believable to me twenty years ago. As a little boy in elementary school, my speech impediment made me the laughingstock of my classmates. Consequently, I never bothered to participate in class. I was unaware back then that God had a plan for me that would shock the socks off my childhood classmates, not to mention me.

I know now that God had control of my life even then. He was preparing me and leading me, opening doors for me so that I could become all I have ever dreamed of becoming, and more. There is an order to life, and life events usually work in some kind of succession. Goals can give your life meaning and direction, placing you in positions and circumstances that eventually allow you to have the kind of successful, fulfilling, and meaningful life you've always wanted. God has a plan for you. But you must be willing to listen, and to follow.

GOALS MUST BE SPECIFIC

This is where you get down to the nitty-gritty and actually write your goals. You've read this section on goal-setting, and you've learned a lot. But, according to statistics, this is where 98 percent of you will quit. When it comes to writing or working toward a goal, most people will not do anything. If you're *really* serious about becoming all that you were created to become, stick with me and do as I suggest in the following pages.

You cannot generalize when it comes to goal-setting. This is a great mistake that people make when writing goals. For example, I've heard people say that their main goal in life is to be happy. *There's no such goal as "happy."* Happiness is a by-product of accomplishing one's goals.

Your subconscious understands pictures, not abstract words. If I ask four different people to think of their favorite car, one may picture a Chevy, another a Buick, another a Corvette, and the last an MG. And just as they pictured four different cars, so these same four people will picture four different situations if I should ask them to imagine being "happy." As with cars, happiness means different things to different people. It's an abstract concept.

If you and I have a common goal, and we're working together toward that goal, we have this warm feeling called "happy." Why? Because a person doesn't have to achieve a goal to be happy. For most people, the mere act of working toward a goal can result in happiness. Seeing the steps accomplished, one by one, en route to an end goal is satisfaction and fulfillment in itself.

Before you begin writing your goals, you should ask yourself the following six questions.

1. *Where Am I Today?*

On a sheet of paper, make seven columns—one for the six questions, and six columns representing the six life areas we discussed earlier in this chapter: professional/financial, social, physical, mental/intellectual, family, and spiritual. Answer this question for each of these life areas. In regard to what you really want out of life, where are you financially, socially, physically, etc., today?

Before you can accomplish any goal, you must first take an inventory of where you are now. I can't make an airline reservation to fly to New York City without first telling the ticket agent where I want to fly *from*. It's crucial that you answer this question. Where do you stand right now in all six areas of your life?

2. *What Do I Really Want?*

If I were a magician and could give you anything you asked for, what would it be? What do you want out of life financially, physically, socially, etc. Why don't you have these things?

Probably because you never took time to think about them. As a result, you really don't know. Now's the time to find out.

In each of the six columns on your paper, write down what you really want in each area. When you've finished, rank those items (within areas) in order of importance to you; then concentrate on the number one item. What's the *one* thing you want most in your life in each area? The Apostle Paul didn't say "all these things I dabble in." Rather, I do "this *one* thing" (cf. Phil. 3:13). That one thing then becomes your goal, or your family's goal.

As you prioritize your goals on paper, you'll begin to see that #2 and #3 can become stepping stones to #1. But you can never achieve #1 until you know what it is—until you know exactly what you want out of life for each area of your life.

3. *When Do I Want This Goal Accomplished?*

When asked this question, most people say, "One of these days." A goal can't be a wandering generality. It must have a specific target date or deadline. Target dates must be flexible, however. Many people may reach their deadline without accomplishing their goal. They then become discouraged and frustrated and simply give up. If this should happen to you, be flexible and realistic enough to change your deadline to reflect your new circumstances. That's, of course, unless there's a very good reason why it cannot be changed. This will allow you more time to work on your goal. As a result, you won't experience a sense of failure because you didn't reach that goal on schedule.

One word of caution, however: since one of the advantages of goal-setting is that it keeps you from procrastinating by keeping you on a schedule, you should only change a deadline when absolutely necessary.

Thinking in terms of long-, short-, and intermediate-range goals is a helpful way to approach the question of when you want your goals completed.

a. Long-range goal: Most goals should have a long-range target of five years, because that seems to be the maximum amount of time most people can comfortably handle when planning ahead. Anything beyond five years is usually an objective, not a goal. Your number one goal should be your long-range goal—that thing you're shooting for five years from now.

If you have a financial goal to have $10,000 in savings within five years, then you've already established your long-range financial goal. Perhaps your family goal is to move into a new home in five years, your physical goal is to lose twenty pounds in one year, and your social goal to become involved in at least one additional community/social activity per year (five in five years), etc. In this way, you've established most of your long-range goals.

And remember, each of your long-range goals needs to be written out for all six areas of your life.

b. Short-range goal: If you're going to accomplish your long-range goals, you must have a series of steps which enable you to get there, because big achievements come from a steady progression of small achievements. Each of your short-range goals must be written out for each of the six areas of your life. Not only do short-range goals give you a clear picture of how to get there; they also enable you to experience a sense of achievement and accomplishment as you complete each of them.

If you want a $10,000 savings account within five years, you know you need to save $2,000 per year, $166.67 per month, $38.46 per week, and $5.48 per day. These become your short-range goals. Write them down.

A number of years ago, I met Dr. Wernher Von Braun, the man responsible for launching the United States into space. We were both on a speaking program in Alabama and had a chance to talk after the program.

"Dr. Von Braun," I said, "where were you the day President Kennedy said that we were going to be on the moon in ten years?"

"I was sitting right there in the room with him," he answered.

"What did you do?"

"I almost passed out!" he exclaimed. "I was one of the chief scientists in the space program, and I knew we couldn't make it to the moon. We didn't even have an adequate rocket fuel."

"What did you do, then?"

"I knew the President was serious, so I wrote down 'ten years to the moon.'"

Von Braun realized that if he was to get this country into space, he needed a plan. And so, his very first act was to write down his long-range goal.

During our conversation, Von Braun went on to tell me that after he wrote down the first goal of reaching the moon within ten years, he went on to write down what had to be done within nine years, eight years, seven years, six years, and so on all the way down to what had to be done within the first six months. He knew that if he was to accomplish what the President wanted, he had to develop a certain kind of rocket fuel within six months—a goal which became his first priority.

Five months and seventeen days later, the United States successfully fired a rocket using a newly developed fuel that Von Braun and his team of scientists had developed. His long-range goal was now believable, realistic, and possible. Within only a few months, he had experienced success on his first short-range goal. Most of us never get that far.

Von Braun then called President Kennedy and said, "Mr. President, we'll be on the moon within ten years!"

c. Intermediate goal: An intermediate goal is the halfway point between your first short-range goal and your long-range goal. It serves as a checkpoint to let you know if you're still on target, and consequently, whether or not you need to make adjustments and changes in order to accomplish your long-range goal. If changes are necessary, the deadline may have to be changed as well.

If you're trying to save for that $10,000 savings account, then within 2.5 years you should have $5,000 in savings. If you don't, you either need to change your deadline, or increase the amount you're saving in order to meet your target date.

On its bicentennial birthday, July 4, 1976, the United States was supposed to land a space probe on Mars. It had been launched nearly two years earlier. About halfway between Earth and Mars, the space engineers and scientists announced that the target was going to be missed. The rocket was veering off course and would probably pass Mars if nothing was done.

Did they give up on that multimillion-dollar project and let it pass Mars? Of course not! They fired on-board retro-rockets in such a way as to put the rocket back on course. They made what is known in the space industry as a mid-course correction, which allowed the rocket to land on Mars as originally planned. That's what an intermediate goal is—a mid-course correction to get you back on target.

Keelan[4] recommends that a time line be drawn using hash marks to indicate short-range, intermediate, and long-range goals. This line can give a person a clear picture of his or her goal and the steps it will take to accomplish it.

Where I Am Today			Where I Want to Be	
1986	1987	1989	1991	1993
FIREMAN	LIEUTENANT	CAPTAIN	DIST. CHIEF	CHIEF

Goals are the building blocks from which success is made. They can point you to accomplishment and achievement as nothing else can. But there is a scheme and a plan to setting goals, and it must be adhered to if you want goal-setting to work for you.

4. *To Whom Will This Prove That They Are Right about Me or Wrong about Me?*

People are generally motivated either to live up to others' expectations or prove others wrong in their evaluation of them. If we would just stop and think a few minutes, we could all remember someone at some time in our lives who told us that we would never make it—maybe because of our background, our education, or because they thought we just didn't have what it would take. These people may have had good intentions and wanted us to be realistic and not dream big dreams that would someday disappoint us. But they said it, nevertheless.

Or perhaps we're trying to prove someone right about us.

Maybe Aunt Sally told you she knew that you'd be president of your company someday. And so, you're working hard to prove her right. She had faith and confidence in you. You want others to see that she knew what she was talking about. If you can write down the name of someone who believes in you, and tell yourself that you want to prove that person right (in order to make him or her proud of you), you'll have the power to pay the price to get what you dreamed for. The next time you're hurting, discouraged, or depressed, look at the name(s) you've written down. You can draw strength and courage from just knowing that there's one person out there who knows you're worthwhile. Hearing someone you love say, "I knew you could do it," gives you the fighting courage to continue on and makes the fight worth the price.

5. *How Will I Know When I've Achieved This Goal?*

Goals must be measurable and tangible. You can't set a goal of "I want to lose some weight," or "I want to improve my grades." Neither are measurable. If there's no way to measure a goal, how will you know when you've achieved it? Goals should determine *how much* you want as well as *what* you want.

Rewriting the above goals as "I will lose ten pounds within six months," and "I will raise my grade point average one point by the end of the next grading period," makes them measurable and tangible. The person writing such goals will know for certain when he has or has not achieved them.

If my goal was to be the number one father in Austin, Texas, next year, how would I know when I've achieved it? I wouldn't know because it's immeasurable and intangible. But if I modified that goal to say that I want my three children to gather at my home on January 1, 1987, and tell me that I'm the greatest father in the world, then I would have a measurable, tangible goal. By being specific about goals, you paint a picture in your subconscious mind that enables you to work toward those goals; and you'll know for certain when you've achieved them.

I once conducted a series of workshops for a frozen foods company in New York. A young man approached me after one of the sessions.

"Are you for real?" he asked.

"Well, I certainly hope so!" I answered, somewhat surprised by his question.

"Boy, I wish I could believe you," he continued. "But I don't think what you say works. So, I'm going to put you to the test."

"Fine," I answered. "Send me your written goals."

About ten days later I received his list. This man was only twenty-two years old and had written a goal to become the general manager of a new plant that was yet to be built. Also, he planned to obtain that position within three years. I knew that the position required that he go through a special school that trained people to become managers of frozen food plants. Only one of these schools existed at the time, located at Florida State University.

This young man didn't have the experience required to get the position without training, or the money needed for tuition to Florida State. His goal was simply to walk into the company president's office and tell him what he wanted. The president would then agree to *pay his tuition,* thus allowing him to go to school for the necessary training. He also had a goal, whereby the president of the company would volunteer full salary and expenses during the time he was in school. Unrealistic?

When I read this list of goals, I thought, "Are these goals, or are these dreams? Is he kidding?"

He went on to tell me in his letter how he pictured the president's office—the desk, the rug, the color of the walls, the pictures that were hanging there. He had a clear picture in his mind of what and how he wanted it to happen.

Two years later, his company asked me to come back and conduct another session, this time in the Catskill Mountains. I drove up a narrow, winding road, through tall multicolored trees, looking for a little hotel nestled among the autumn splendor. I walked into the meeting room filled with company employees. My eyes darted about as I tried to spot the young man who wanted to be a plant manager. I didn't see him. *I hope no one asks me about him,* I thought to myself.

About five minutes before I began the session, someone walked up behind me and said, "Lewis! How are you?"

Turning around, I discovered my young friend. "I was looking for you," I said.

I couldn't wait to hear his explanation for why he hadn't become plant manager. I knew the company president then. I couldn't see him paying tuition for anyone who hadn't proved himself yet—let alone full salary and expenses while the employee was in school. It wasn't realistic to me . . . but it *was* realistic to my young friend.

"Guess where I've been?" he said, a broad smile creeping across his face.

"I don't know," I answered, wary of the response I was about to get.

"Florida State University! Can you stay over an extra day? I'd like you to come and see the new plant we're opening on Monday—the plant I'm going to manage."

This story taught me a great lesson about doubting anyone's goals! You see, my friend knew exactly what he wanted—he wrote it down, fixed a picture of it in his mind, and then went after it. You must establish specific, believable, realistic, measurable, and tangible goals. And then you must fix them in your mind before you can take the necessary steps to accomplish them.

When Florence Chadwick first tried to swim the twenty-one-mile-wide English Channel, she came within three miles of reaching the French shore. There and then she grew exhausted and quit. As she neared her goal, a thick fog set in over the Strait of Dover, blinding her view of the shore. She later asked her crew how close she had come to land.

When they told her she had come within three miles, she responded, "I could have made three more miles if I could have only seen the shore."

Florence Chadwick depended on clear weather that day, not to mention that she didn't have her goal fixed in her *mind*. I can't emphasize enough how important this is. You need to have a physical picture of your goal in your mind (a new home, yourself in "thinner" days, etc.); then you must visualize it often. This is what will keep you working toward your ultimate achievement.

6. *Why Do I Want This?*

It's not what you want out of life but *why* you want it that makes the difference. The *why* is the element that lights the spark, giving you the energy you need to accomplish a given goal.

When my first son was born, I was making $250 a month at Goodyear Tire in Stamford. That wasn't a bad salary in those days. We weren't wealthy, but we were doing all right. But, I had dreams and desires for myself and my family that went beyond Goodyear Tire.

Then a banker friend began telling the local insurance companies that Lewis Timberlake had what it takes and that they ought to hire me. He sent nine companies to interview me! I mean, this man had faith in yours truly. Every single company offered me at least $1,000 a month starting salary. I was only twenty-four years old and thought I'd died and gone to heaven. I had been offered four times my current salary. I couldn't believe it.

This is the kind of opportunity that most young husbands and fathers would grab up in a second. But I had to think things through. Doing so, I discovered one problem. There were nineteen insurance men in Stamford—a town with a population of only three thousand people. On top of that, none of those men were doing very well. I figured if these men—older, smarter, more experienced than I—couldn't make it, how could I? So I decided to stay right where I was and make it rather than take a new job and fail. I needed the security more than I needed the money. So, I turned down all the offers.

A few months later, a gentleman from yet a tenth insurance company called and asked if he could meet with me. We went down to the local cafe, grabbed a corner booth, ordered some coffee, and began to talk.

"Lewis, I like what I've been hearing about you," he began. "Why don't you tell me about yourself in your own words."

After listening to my story, he asked, "If I could do anything in the world for you right now, if there's one thing in life that I could give you, what would it be? What is the one thing you want now above everything else?"

I gave him the perfect universal answer: "I don't know!"

"Think about it for a minute," he responded.

"Anything at all?" I asked.

"Anything," he answered.

"I'd like to buy my wife a piano."

"Why?"

"Well, you won't believe this," I said, "but the first time I asked my wife to marry me, she said no. Can you believe that?"

I went on to tell him about how I knew Georgia Ann loved me. After all, we'd discussed our feelings for each other. And so, I couldn't understand why she'd turned me down.

Apparently, she knew that I was going to propose to her. And so, the afternoon before the big date, she went to ask advice from her high school English teacher—someone Georgia Ann held in high respect.

When Georgia Ann asked her teacher if she should marry Lewis Timberlake, the teacher responded, "No, honey, he's never going to amount to anything. I don't think you should."

So Georgia Ann took her advice and said no.

My wife wanted to marry someone who could take care of her, provide for her, and give her security. When she finally agreed to marry me, I had to promise her that I'd provide for her, that I'd take care of her, and that *nothing* would ever come between us.

Looking across the table at this insurance executive, I told him how Georgia Ann thought of a piano as the central focus of a home. It was a source of pleasure around which family and friends could gather to sing and have fellowship. She felt that a home filled with music must be a happy home. It came down to whether I could buy her a piano. That would prove that I meant all those promises about staying together and providing for her. Besides, everyone in Stamford would know that she had married someone special if I could buy her a particular piano that I had seen in a local store window. It was *the* piano of all time. No one else in Stamford had one that could even come close to comparing with it.

"Why don't you buy it for her?" he asked.

"What? On $250 a month? Are you crazy? I could never afford a piano like that. It costs $1,500."

Then he told me that if I would go to work for him and perform a list of specific duties, in twenty-four months he'd give me a bonus check for $1,500. In addition to that, he'd start me off at $1,000 a month right then and there.

Then he pulled an employment agreement out of his briefcase, shoved it in front of me, handed me a pen, and said, "Press hard, Lewis, there are three copies there."

It took me seventeen months, not the prescribed twenty-four, to do what was required of me in the agreement. I received my $1,500 bonus and bought *the* piano for my wife. The day they delivered *the* piano to my home, our old high school English teacher who'd told Georgia Ann that I'd never amount to anything was there sitting in the living room visiting my wife. It was gratifying to prove her wrong!

Abraham Maslow is one of the great authorities on motivation. He states that there are five basic drives motivating people to do the things they do: survival, security, social desires, self-esteem, and self-actualization.[5]

The newest motivational research has condensed these drives into two: to love and be loved, and to feel worthwhile—to ourselves or to someone else. Everything you do is done because you are seeking an end result from one of the above drives. This explains why you work so hard to achieve your goals. If you look deep enough into your heart, you'll usually find one of these reasons as the explanation for why you are setting your goals in the first place. And if you can keep that reason foremost in your thoughts, it will make the promise worth the price.

I didn't go into the insurance business in order to make a $1,500 bonus or to buy a piano. I went into the business because I needed to feel loved and worthwhile. I also needed to be able to prove to my wife that I loved her. I realized this the minute the insurance man showed me *what* I wanted, and *why* I wanted it. It was then that I saw myself as a winner. I had the drive to do what was necessary to achieve my goal.

Years later my family moved to Austin. One day I received a call from a real estate agent who asked if she could meet me in five minutes. She told me she had something to show me. She came to my office in a car as long as my office building. As I approached the car, she got out and opened the door, asking me to get in. I slid into the front seat and looked behind me. Who did I find? It was my wife sitting there, grinning from ear to ear.

"Oh, my soul," I said. "We are *not* going to buy a new house. You understand that, don't you? We have three children in school, and I just started a new business. We can't afford a a new house."

"Yes, dear," she said sweetly.

We were then living in the biggest house I had ever lived in. I thought we were happy there. We didn't *need* a new house.

The real estate agent drove us up into the hills, just west of Austin. We stopped at the top of a hill, in front of an enormous house that looked like it had a hundred and seventeen trees in the front yard. We got out, walked through the trees, and just stood there, looking at a house with majestic white columns parading across its front. Then I felt my wife's hand slowly slip into mine, squeezing it ever so gently.

While Georgia Ann and I were standing there holding hands, the agent walked up on the other side of me and whispered, "I wonder what your old English teacher would say if she could see Georgia Ann living in a house like this?"

Do I have to tell you where we live today? Why did I buy that house for her? Not because I wanted it. I bought it because I wanted to feel loved and worthwhile.

In order for a goal to be specific, you must first ask yourself the above questions (where, what, when, who, how, and why) for each goal in the six life areas. If you go through this process of keeping goals personal, written, continual, compatible, all-encompassing, realistic, and specific, nothing can stop you from becoming what you want to become and from having the things in life that you want to have.

Paul Brouwer writes,

> It is not enough, however, just to see ourselves as we are now. Such understanding is a necessary starting point, or basis on which to build. But we must also see what our real selves *could* be, and grow into that.[6]

The ability to see yourself as you *can* be provides the motivation you need to complete the final step in your goal-setting program.

GOALS MUST BE WORKABLE

In order for a goal to be a goal and not a wish or a dream, you must have a picture in your mind of that goal; then you must have a plan for its accomplishment. The plan makes it workable, and therefore, achievable.

Each week in my seminars, I tell literally hundreds of stories about people just like you and me who, after they began writing down their goals and action plans, eventually became all that they ever dreamed of becoming. The main difference between a winner and a loser is that winners set goals and work toward them—they are willing to do what it takes to achieve their dreams and goals.

1. *Obstacles*. In developing your action plan, you first need to list all the obstacles that stand between you and your goal. Maybe you've had a dream of owning a farm someday; hence, you'd like to make that your long-range goal. What stands in your way? Money? Education? Time? How can you solve these problems if you don't take the time to list them and work out ways to overcome them?

In chapter 3 we discussed how the self-image, through the subconscious mind, controls our behavior. Your self-image has nothing whatsoever to do with your potential—what you have the talent, ability, and capacity to become in life. However, it does have everything to do with your behavior, performance, and reactions to situations and events around you. Therefore, if in your subconscious you believe something is a problem or an obstacle, even though it may not be a problem, then it's a problem to you. (Remember, you can't lie to yourself.)

Listing the obstacles that stand between you and your goals forces you to put down on paper and *see all the reasons why you don't have what you want to have in life.*

I'd just finished a seminar in Florida when a gentleman rushed up to me and exclaimed, "I want you to know I thought your seminar was marvelous, but I can't do what you say."

"Why not?" I asked.

"My dream all my life has been to be a lawyer."

"Great!" I said. "Then why don't you go back to college and become a lawyer?"

"I can't!" he exclaimed. "I just told you that."

He went on to tell me how he fell in love and got married while in college. They'd had their first child before he graduated, and have had several children since. Now he was forty years old, and felt he could never become what he'd always dreamed of becoming.

"I have a great idea!" I told him. "Why don't you go to law school part time?"

"What? Are you crazy? It would take me four years or more to get my degree. I'd be at least forty-four years old by then."

"How old will you be in four years if you *don't* go back to school?" I asked him.

This leads us beyond merely describing what your problem/obstacle is. The next question is: What are you going to do to solve it? Are you willing to do those things that unsuccessful people won't do?

2. *Ways to Overcome Obstacles*. Once you have each obstacle listed, make a list of things that you can do to overcome them. This becomes your first list of goals, because you must overcome the obstacles *first*. If you want to buy a farm and your main obstacle is education, perhaps you can go back to school at night to learn more about farming or complete a degree in agriculture. If the second obstacle is money, maybe you can begin looking for another job that pays more, etc. Do this for each obstacle on your list.

I used to do a series of programs for a secretaries' association in Texas. Each year we'd have about five hundred young women participate in the program. After one of these programs, I returned to my office. The phone rang. My secretary was out at the time, so I answered it.

"Is this Lewis Timberlake?" a distinctly female voice asked.

"Yes, it is."

"Mr. Timberlake, do you really believe in what you say?"

I've heard that question so many times over the years, that I'm never surprised when I hear it again.

"Yes, ma'am, I really believe it," I answered.

"I'm going to write my goals and send them to you. Would you call me back and tell me if they are achievable?"

"No," I answered. "I'll call and tell you if you've written them correctly. But you must remember, if they're written correctly and you believe them, you can achieve them. It's up to you, not me."

She agreed to that. In a few days I received her goals in the mail. She was forty-seven years old and had never been married. Guess what her goal was? She said that she was unhappy being alone, and that her number one goal was to get married.

This one really threw me for a loop. In all my years of conducting seminars on goal-setting, this particular goal had never come up before. I really didn't know how to handle it.

I picked up the phone and called the president of the secretaries' association. I asked her if she knew this lady. When she said she did, I then asked her to tell me a little bit about her.

As it turned out, she wasn't an attractive woman and had a hard time getting along with people. As a matter of fact, my friend described her as "crabby." I thanked her for her help; then I started wondering how I was going to help this woman who wanted to get married, but whom no one liked.

Going back over her goals list, I could see that she'd written them out exactly the way I'd taught. Then I got to her list of obstacles. Her number one obstacle: "I'm not very pretty." Her second obstacle: "No one finds me easy to get along with." Her third obstacle: "I'm not attractive in clothes because I have a terrible figure." She knew what her obstacles were. No one had to tell her.

Following her list of obstacles was a list of things that she could do to overcome them. She wanted to sign up for a course in a local department store where she would learn makeup, grooming, and fashion—the kind of course that teaches you how to maximize your assets and minimize your liabilities. The next thing she listed was a plan to enroll in a local beauty college so she could learn to fix her own hair. Her third plan was to sign up for a membership in a local health club where she could exercise daily and learn good diet and weight control habits. She also planned to enroll in a course in human relations in the local community college.

I wrote to her and told her that she had done exactly as she should have in writing down her goals; then I wished her luck and told her that I looked forward to seeing her at the seminar the next year.

One year later, I walked into the Marriott Hotel and surveyed the crowd of five hundred secretaries. Sitting in the middle of this throng of women was one lone man. In those days male secretaries were rare. Having aroused my curiosity, I decided to meet this man and find out a little about him.

As I reached out to shake hands with him, the lady sitting next to him pulled on my pants leg and said, "Mr. Timberlake, could I hug your neck?"

I'm in favor of things like that, so I said, "Sure!"

She stood up and hugged me, and then she said, "I want you to meet my husband."

"You're responsible for this, you know," he said.

Uh-oh! What had I done?

"You don't know me, do you?" she asked.

"No, I guess I don't," I responded.

She proceeded to explain that she was the lady who had called me and sent me her goals list the year before. She was the lady who wanted to get married. I couldn't believe it. She was a very attractive woman. She didn't look at all like the person my friend had described to me.

"I brought my husband to meet you. You see, if I hadn't attended your seminar, I would never have known that I have a right to be someone special. We wouldn't be married today. We're here because we just wanted to thank you."

She stood up in front of 498 women that day and told her story.

"If I had never gotten married," she said, "it still would have been worth it, because now I like who I am."

Obviously, I didn't do that. She did. I just showed her *how* she could do it. Goal-setting isn't mysterious or magic. It's simply putting together a picture of what you want, why you want it, the reasons why you don't have it, and a plan of action for achieving it. That way, you're prepared when opportunities open up for you—you're ready to take action to become all you were created to be. No one can achieve your goals for you. Only you can do that.

When I was a child growing up in Stamford, a friend of my family was a brilliant artist. Everyone who had seen his work believed that he was destined to become one of the great artists of our time. He would stand and paint, talking to children while he worked. As he spoke, his words seemed to be transformed onto the canvas right before our very eyes.

He spoke many times about creating his one great masterpiece. But each time a friend or neighbor would ask about it, he'd always reply with such ready answers as, "I didn't get around to it today—maybe tomorrow"; "I didn't feel like painting today—maybe tomorrow"; "The weather wasn't right today—maybe tomorrow"; or "A friend dropped by today—maybe tomorrow." He talked about what he would do "tomorrow" until the day he died.

On the day of his funeral, all his friends paid their last respects. They listened to his eulogy, they sang hymns, and they said a last prayer for their friend. At the cemetery, his friends watched as they lowered him into his final resting place—a place accompanied by his lost hopes and dreams. And before they filed away from the grave, they read the words engraved on his tombstone—words chosen by a poet who knew him well:

> He was going to be all that a man could be—
> Tomorrow.
> None will be stronger or braver than he—
> Tomorrow.
> If a friend was troubled and weary he knew,
> And he wanted some help and needed it, too,
> On him he would call and see what he could do—
> Tomorrow.
> All the greatest of mortals could have been—
> Tomorrow.
> The world would have known him had he only seen—
> Tomorrow.

But the fact is he died and faded from view,
And all that was left when living was through
Was a mountain of things he intended to do—
Tomorrow.

He always talked about the obstacles that stood between him and his masterpiece and about what he would do tomorrow. But he never actually *did* anything to overcome the obstacles. You see, the "obstacles" were only in his mind. He didn't really believe that he could create a masterpiece. He didn't believe in himself enough to actually *do* whatever was necessary to accomplish his dream.

Once you've removed the obstacles that stand between you and your goals, you can then begin to work on achieving them. Dare to dream! There's no greater feeling than that sense of accomplishment that comes as each goal is realized. Remember Yogi Berra's words of caution: "If you don't know where you're going in life, you'll probably end up somewhere else!" Start now to develop action plans for your goals, because goals are simply dreams until you commit yourself to do something about them.

If you'll look to God for direction, he'll open doors for you that you never dreamed possible. He may also shut a few doors. If this happens, reexamine your goals and their importance to you and your family. Read the promises in Psalms 32:8, 37:23, and 73:24. And remember the promise made in Isaiah 42:16: "He will bring blind Israel along a path they have not seen before. He will make the darkness bright before them and smooth and straighten out the road ahead. He will not forsake them" (TLB).

Some people look backward and say, "If only I had done this or that." Goal-setters look forward and say, "What can I do next?" *Anyone can be a winner!*

EPILOGUE

"EARTHWORMS FOR SALE"

My beloved high school teacher, Ma Crockett, told me a story once that she wanted me to carry with me for the rest of my life. It impressed me so that I've never forgotten it.

A beautiful little Blue Jay flew high in the sky, proud of its plumage and beauty, knowing that as it flew, all eyes were turned on it. This little Blue Jay was without a doubt the most admired bird in its community.

One day the little bird flew low, close to the tree tops. As he flew in and out among the trees, he spied a man dressed in black strolling down a little country lane.

"Earthworms for sale. Earthworms for sale," the old man sang.

The little Blue Jay thought, "Oh, how I love earthworms! I wonder how much they are."

Lighting on the old man's shoulder, the little bird asked, "How much do you want for your earthworms?"

"Oh, they're cheap," the old man answered. "Just one feather for one worm."

"Oh, how I love earthworms," the little bird thought. "No one would notice one little feather missing."

He plucked out one of his beautiful blue feathers and handed it to the old man in return for a delicious earthworm. Then he soared into the clouds, happy and content.

The following day the Blue Jay heard the old man again singing his song, "Earthworms for sale. Earthworms for sale."

"Oh, how I love earthworms," the little bird thought. "That worm tasted so good yesterday, and no one even noticed that I had a feather missing. Maybe I'll have just one more."

So again he plucked a feather and traded it for another earthworm.

The same scene was repeated the next day, and the next, and the next—until he had plucked one feather too many. After he'd purchased a final earthworm, he could no longer soar into the sky. No matter how hard he flapped his wings, no matter how high he jumped, he couldn't catch the wind in his remaining feathers. He was so dejected over what he'd done, that he crawled into the tall grass beside the road and died.

Another Blue Jay flying overhead found his little friend, buried him under a giant oak tree, and placed the following epitaph on his headstone:

Here lies a poor lost Blue Jay,
Hush your note each bird that sings.
Here lies a poor foolish Blue Jay,
Who for earthworms sold his wings.

The secret to becoming a winner is realizing that everyone is born to be successful, and that you have a right to that success. It means refusing to "sell your feathers"—accepting less and less from life until you finally settle for mediocrity or second best. It's knowing that you should never give up trying to achieve your dreams. It's being unafraid of failure, because you know that the only time you can't afford to fail is the very last time you try.

The secret to becoming a winner is knowing that you can be whatever you were created to be. It's knowing that, like the Hereford cattle, you can walk directly into the wind and meet life's storms head-on with fortitude, courage, and faith. It's realizing that it's never too late to begin again, that it's never too late to rise above the ashes of defeat. You *can* accept responsibility for your mistakes, concentrate on the positives, and get on with your life. It's seeing yourself as a winner and acting like it's so when it's not so in order for it to be so.

The secret to becoming a winner is understanding that you have the power and the ability to change the way you see yourself. It's realizing that your self-image has nothing whatsoever to do with your potential but everything to do with your performance. It's programming yourself with positive and constructive thoughts, ideas, books, and tapes. It's reliving your successes, accomplishments, awards, victories, and triumphs in life. It's capitalizing on your assets. It's realizing that you've been created as someone uniquely different, as someone who has something worthwhile to offer the world.

The secret to becoming a winner is understanding that circumstances don't control your life unless you let them. Rather, it's how you *react* to those circumstances that makes all the difference. It's eliminating self-pity and associating with other winners. It's taking charge of your life by setting goals to work toward using those road maps that point you to success. It's understanding that it is never too late to do the things that unsuccessful people won't do. And in doing those things, it's remembering never, never to hurt anyone else or compromise your own beliefs and convictions in the process.

The secret to becoming a winner is getting to know yourself and liking what you find. It's knowing with all your heart that you are unique and special, that God gave you talents and abilities in a combination unlike anyone else's. It's laying claim to all those talents and abilities you've been blessed with. It's settling for nothing less than God's best for you.

For forty years after their escape from Egypt, the Israelites wandered through an arid desert, failing to take possession of God's gift to them—the Promised Land. Through disobedience, disbelief, and indifference, they settled for second best. They couldn't enjoy what they didn't possess. Do you have God-given talents that you haven't claimed? Do you have special gifts and abilities that you haven't taken possession of? What are you waiting for? *Anyone can be a winner!*

Good luck, and may God bless you.

NOTES

Introduction
1. Dr. Maxwell Maltz, *The Magic Power of Self-image Psychology* (New York: Pocket Books, a division of Simon & Schuster, Inc., 1970), p. vi.
2. *Ibid.*
3. Maltz, *Psycho-Cybernetics & Self-fulfillment* (New York: Grosset & Dunlap, 1970), p. 30.

Chapter 2
1. Frank B. Minirth, M.D. and Paul D. Meier, M.D., *Happiness Is a Choice* (Grand Rapids, Mich.: Baker Book House, 1978), p. 168.
2. Lewis Carroll, *The Annotated Alice: Alice's Adventures in Wonderland & Through the Looking Glass* (New York: Bramhall House, 1960), p. 88.
3. Arthur Miller, *Death of a Salesman* (New York: The Viking Press, 1949, 1977), p. 138.

Chapter 3
1. Dr. Maxwell Maltz, *The Magic Power of Self-image Psychology* (New York: Pocket Books, a division of Simon & Schuster, Inc., 1970), p. 62.
2. *Ibid.*, p. 63.

Chapter 4
1. "Winston tastes good like a cigarette should."
2. "Pepsi Cola hits the spot."
3. "Lucky Strike means fine tobacco."
4. Dr. Maxwell Maltz, *The Magic Power of Self-image Psychology* (New York: Pocket Books, a division of Simon & Schuster, Inc., 1970), p. 16.

Chapter 5
1. Dr. James Keelan, *Having Fun Being Yourself* (Arvada, Colo.: Communications Unlimited, 1975), p. 59. Used with permission.
2. *Ibid.,* pp. 59, 60.
3. Dr. Maxwell Maltz, *The Magic Power of Self-image Psychology* (New York: Pocket Books, a division of Simon & Schuster, Inc., 1970), p. 149.
4. *Ibid.,* p. 24.

Chapter 7
1. Betty Hassler, "Humility: Putting Life in Perspective," *Home Bible Study Guide* (Nashville, Tenn.: Sunday School Board of the Southern Baptist Convention), Vol. 6, No. 9, pp. 10, 11. All rights reserved. Used by permission.
2. *Ibid.,* p. 9.

Chapter 8
1. Dr. James Dobson, *Hide or Seek* (Old Tappan, N.J.: Fleming H. Revell Co., 1974), p. 158.

Chapter 9
1. "One Solitary Life," author unknown.

Chapter 11
1. Don Fearheiley, "Finetuning: Selfhood," *Home Bible Study Guide* (Nashville, Tenn.: Sunday School Board of the Southern Baptist Convention), Vol. 6, No. 12, p. 25. All rights reserved. Used by permission.
2. *Ibid.*
3. "Trivial Pursuit," copyright © 1981 (Bay Shore, N.Y.: Horn Abbot Ltd., Selchow & Righter Co.).
4. Dr. James Keelan, *Having Fun Being Yourself* (Arvada, Colo.: Communications Unlimited, 1975), p. 169. Used with permission.
5. *The Third Force: The Psychology of Abraham Maslow* (New York: Pocket Books, a division of Simon & Schuster, Inc., 1970), p. 52.
6. Paul J. Brouwer, "The Power to See Ourselves," *Harvard Business Review,* Vol. 42, No. 6, 1964, pp. 156ff.

BIBLIOGRAPHY

Associated Press & Grolier Enterprises. *Pursuit of Excellence: The Olympic Story*. Danbury, Conn.: Grolier Enterprises, Inc., 1979.

Berne, Dr. Eric. *Games People Play*. New York: Ballantine Books, 1978.

Bristol, Claude M. *The Magic of Believing*. Englewood Cliffs, N.J.: Prentice-Hall, 1948, 1976.

Brouwer, Paul J. "The Power to See Ourselves." *Harvard Business Review*. Vol. 42, No. 6. Boston, Mass.: November/December, 1964.

Carnegie, Dale. *How to Stop Worrying and Start Living*. New York: Simon & Schuster, 1944.

Carroll, Lewis. *The Annotated Alice: Alice's Adventures in Wonderland & Through the Looking Glass*. New York: Bramhall House, 1960.

Dobson, Dr. James. *Hide or Seek*. Old Tappan, N.J.: Fleming H. Revell Co., 1974.

Dodson, Dr. Fitzhugh. *The You That Could Be*. Chicago, Ill.: Follett Publishing Co., 1976.

Edwards, William E. *Ten Days to a Great New Life*. Englewood Cliffs, N.J.: Prentice-Hall, 1963.

Fearheiley, Don. "Finetuning: Selfhood," *Home Bible Study Guide*. Volume 6, No. 12, Nashville, Tenn.: Sunday School Board of the Southern Baptist Convention, September, 1984.

Fosdick, Harry Emerson. *On Being a Real Person*. New York: Harper Brothers, 1943.

BIBLIOGRAPHY

Glasser, William. *Positive Addiction*. New York: Harper & Row, 1976.
Glasser, William. *Schools Without Failure*. New York: Harper & Row, 1969.
Goble, Frank. *Excellence in Leadership*. Naperville, Ill.: Caroline House Publishers, 1972.
Goble, Frank. *The Third Force: The Psychology of Abraham Maslow*. New York: Pocket Books. Published by arrangement with Grossman Publishers, Inc., 1970.
Gunther, Max. *The Very, Very Rich and How They Got That Way*. Chicago, Ill.: Playboy Paperbacks, 1973.
Hassler, Betty. "Humility: Putting Life in Perspective," *Home Bible Study Guide*, Volume 6, No. 9. Nashville, Tenn.: Sunday School Board of the Southern Baptist Convention, June 1984.
James, Muriel, and Jongewar, Dorothy. *Born to Win*. New York: New American Library, 1978.
Jongeward, Dr. Dorothy. *Everybody Wins*. Reading, Mass.: Addison-Wesley, 1976.
Keelan, Dr. James. *Having Fun Being Yourself*. Arvada, Colo.: Communications Unlimited, 1975.
Kieran, John, and Daley, Arthur. *The Story of the Olympic Games. 776 B.C.—1956 A.D.* Philadelphia, Penn.: J.B. Lippincott Co., 1957.
Maltz, Dr. Maxwell. *Creative Living for Today*. New York: Prentice-Hall, 1967.
Maltz, Dr. Maxwell. *The Magic Power of Self-image Psychology*. New York: Pocket Books, 1970. Pocket Book edition published by arrangement with Prentice-Hall, 1964.
Maltz, Dr. Maxwell. *Psycho-Cybernetics & Self-fulfillment*. New York: Grossett & Dunlap, 1970.
Maslow, Abraham. *Motivation and Personality*. New York: Harper & Row Publishers, Inc., 1954.
Maslow, Abraham. *Toward a Psychology of Being*. Litten Educational Publishing, Inc., 1968.
Miller, Arthur. *Death of a Salesman*. New York: Viking Press, 1949, 1977.
Minirth, Frank B., M.D., and Meier, Paul D., M.D. *Happiness Is a Choice*. Grand Rapids, Mich.: Baker Book House, 1978.
Narramore, Bruce. *You're Someone Special*. Grand Rapids, Mich.: Zondervan Publishing House, 1978.
Parker Editorial Staff. *The Parker Prosperity Program*. West Nyack, N.Y.: Parker Publishing Co., 1967.
Peale, Dr. Norman Vincent. *Enthusiasm Makes the Difference*. New York: Prentice-Hall, 1967.
Peale, Dr. Norman Vincent. *Stay Alive All Your Life*. New York: Prentice-Hall, 1957.
Peale, Dr. Norman Vincent. *The Tough-minded Optimist*. New York: Prentice-Hall, 1961.
Peale, Dr. Norman Vincent. *You Can If You Think You Can*. New York: Fawcett Crest Books, 1974.
Rogers, Carl R. *On Becoming a Person*. Boston, Mass.: Houghton Mifflin Company, 1961.
Rogers, Carl R. *A Way of Being*. Boston Mass.: Houghton Mifflin Company, 1980.
Schuller, Robert H. *Self-love*. New York: A Jove Book, Berkley Publishing Group, 1969.

Toffler, Alvin. *Future Shock*. New York: A Bantam Book, Random House, Inc., 1970.

"Trivial Pursuit." Bay Shore, New York: Horn Abbot Ltd., Selchow & Righter Co., 1981.

Wagner, Maurice E. *The Sensation of Being Somebody: Building an Adequate Self-concept*. Grand Rapids, Mich.: Zondervan Publishing House, 1975.

Ziglar, Zig. *See You at the Top*. Gretna, La.: Pelican Publishing Co., Inc., 1975.

For information about Lewis Timberlake's seminars, cassette tapes, and newsletter, write or call
Timberlake & Associates, Inc.
P.O. Box 1571
Austin, Texas 78767-1571
(512) 458-2531